BASIC
SELF-
KNOWLEDGE

BASIC SELF-KNOWLEDGE

HARRY BENJAMIN

Samuel Weiser, Inc.
York Beach, Maine

First published in 1971 by
Samuel Weiser, Inc.
Box 612
York Beach, Maine 03910

Eighth printing, 1989

ISBN 0-87728-162-9

Printed in the United States of America by
Edwards Brothers, Inc.

To B.P., with gratitude.

HARRY BENJAMIN, N.D.

PREFACE

THE sole purpose in writing this book is to present its subject in as simple a form as possible, in the hope that it will interest people who might otherwise not have been brought into touch with this important subject. It is an *introduction* to the subject of esoteric psychology and the writer is conscious of its limitations. Nevertheless, it is his hope that many may be encouraged to take up the study of self-knowledge more deeply, to their everlasting benefit. Enough has been said to enable the reader to become sufficiently prepared to go forward with his or her studies under more competent direction than the writer himself could give.

The main object of the present book is to deal with the system of esoteric development first expounded by the Russian, Gurdjieff. He brought it before the Western World. His pupil and co-worker Ouspensky formulated the system after being instructed in it by Gurdjieff. The late Dr. Maurice Nicoll commented on the system in his *Psychological Commentaries on the Teachings of Gurdjieff and Ouspensky,* having been a personal pupil of both. Dr. Nicoll had nothing whatever to do with the system's origination or its formulation, yet we wish to emphasize that it is essentially Dr. Nicoll's *Psychological Commentaries* which form the basis of the ideas put forward in our discussion of the Gurdjieff system. They offer the widest possible view of the system, in its many-sided and varied aspects, to those who have never come into direct contact with the works of Gurdjieff and Ouspensky, nor had personal instruction from them.

H. B.

CONTENTS

Chapter		Page
	PREFACE	6
	INTRODUCTION	9
I	MAN KNOW THYSELF	15
II	THE WAY TO SELF-KNOWLEDGE	21
III	IMAGINARY "I"	29
IV	SELF-OBSERVATION	35
V	SELF-REMEMBERING	41
VI	SELF-JUSTIFYING	45
VII	PERSONALITY AND ESSENCE	50
VIII	MAN AS A SELF-DEVELOPING ORGANISM	59
IX	NEGATIVE EMOTIONS	65
X	INTERNAL AND EXTERNAL ACCOUNTS	71
XI	INNER TALKING: ATTITUDES: AND PICTURES	77
XII	LEVELS OF BEING	83
XIII	METANOIA	91
XIV	THE FOUR STATES OF CONSCIOUSNESS	100
XV	MAN AND THE COSMOS	104
XVI	THE LIMITATIONS OF LOGICAL THINKING	118
XVII	THREE UNIVERSAL FORCES	131
XVIII	GAINING AND LOSING FORCE	136
XIX	TIME AND ETERNITY	142
XX	A CHAPTER ON KRISHNAMURTI	151
XXI	IS IT WORTH IT?	161

"This work is beautiful when you see why it exists and what it means. It is about liberation. It is as beautiful as if, locked for years in prison, you see a stranger entering who offers you a key. But you may refuse it because you have acquired prison-habits and have forgotten your origin, which is from the stars."

MAURICE NICOLL,

Psychological Commentaries on the Teachings of Gurdjieff and Ouspensky.

INTRODUCTION

WE live in an age wherein material values seem to predominate almost exclusively, and wherein religion (taken in its broadest sense) seems to be fighting a losing battle. Orthodox creeds of all kinds are retreating before the onslaught of the combined forces of Materialism and "Science". Underneath, however, there can be discerned a current at work which indicates that many people are completely dissatisfied with things as they are, and are genuinely seeking for a way of life which is more satisfying than that offered by current thought, whether Materialistic, Scientific, or Religious. In short, these people find themselves outside the ranks either of the religiously orthodox or unorthodox, or of the scientifically orthodox or unorthodox. They feel they cannot side with those who are following the path of orthodoxy, whether it has to do with Religion or Anti-Religion (backed up by modern Scientific Materialism). Such people are seeking for a deeper motive for existence than they have hitherto come across. They seek, and find this and that which attracts them. Something really satisfying, however, which can give their lives REAL MEANING AND PURPOSE, they cannot seem to discover.

In his book *The Outsider*, which created such a sensation when it was first published, the young author Colin Wilson put forward a viewpoint which is extremely to the point. He showed that throughout modern literature there runs a thread of thought which indicates that there exists a class of people who find ordinary life meaningless and purposeless. These people feel instinctively that there *must* be some other way of

9

living with more scope and purpose for existence than that
which people generally follow, whether it be the path of conventional orthodoxy with regard to Religion, or the path of
conventional unorthodoxy of Scientific Materialism. Both
trends have become conventional and indeed orthodox in their
respective ways, and both are found wanting by the class of
people referred to in Wilson's book. He terms such people
"Outsiders", because they stand outside of present-day life,
because they see through the shams of both the orthodox and
unorthodox viewpoints, and realize that life has to be lived far
more deeply if it is to mean anything at all. In other words,
these "Outsiders" have come to realize that life today is far
too shallow, no matter what camp one may be in, whether of
the right or left, or of the orthodox or unorthodox.

Wilson gives a tentative answer, saying that what we need
is a return to religion; but not the religion of orthodoxy, which
has proved unsatisfying to many earnest seekers after truth
and understanding. A religion which satisfies man's deepest
cravings and which puts him in real touch with the deeper
truths of the Universe, is needed. Wilson goes further and
points to the work of the Russian, Gurdjieff, as being significant in regard to this question; but in the writer's opinion
Wilson does not go far enough. He leaves off where the real
quest should begin. He points in the right direction, as it
were, but then stops in order to make out that Shaw provides
the answer to the questings of the outsider. In Shaw, however,
we cannot find that which the outsider is seeking, i.e., a way
of life which is truly religious in the sense of bringing him
into direct touch with Universal Truth and Being; Shaw's
theory of the Life Force is merely an intellectualisation. It
exists only in the mind; it has no validity beyond that, i.e.,
in reality.

People think that if they study a subject, they understand
it. Creative living (i.e., dynamic living) is one of the things
about which a vast amount of thinking is done in the belief

that by thinking about it one is living creatively. In our view Colin Wilson falls into this very category, and so inevitably does his solution of the problem of the outsider. Creative living is really the aim and purpose of true religion, if one understands religion in its deepest sense : of living in accordance with, and in relation to, the basic laws of one's being. Many people will no doubt query whether such laws exist, but unless one is ready to accept the idea that they do, at first merely as an hypothesis, until tested and proved for oneself, then no possibility will exist for turning in the right direction for the achievement of the purpose of real living in a world which does not understand what this means. To be really religious means to be truly creative, i.e., to live in such a way that one's innate powers are developed in accordance with the basic laws of one's real nature. That can only come about through an entirely different approach to life and to ourselves from that current today, whether one is living along orthodox or unorthodox lines, religious, materialistic, scientific, or otherwise.

We said earlier that Wilson mentions the name of the Russian, Gurdjieff, in his book *The Outsider,* as one who can throw light on the subject of the true meaning of existence, and there is another who has tended to turn men's minds in the same direction—although from a somewhat different angle —and that is the Hindu, Krishnamurti. The talks and writings of Krishnamurti reveal an attitude to life and living which is fundamentally divergent from the commonly accepted outlook. When one reads what he has to say, one has the feeling of entering an entirely different world of thought and meaning, utterly foreign to that in which one is living. Krishnamurti exposes the fallacies which underlie ordinary living, and which make that living so sterile and unsatisfying. If we begin to understand what he is saying, we come to realise that all our values and viewpoints are completely fallacious. The latter have been the cause of our inability to live properly, and account for why we find life thoroughly unsatisfactory as regards the deeper aspects of living and what it means. We may be satisfied superficially with life at times, and in certain directions, but those of us who think and feel deeply are quite aware of the fact that basically we are *not* satisfied with life as we are living it, and would be glad to find a way to change direction towards something far more satisfying and rewarding.

Krishnamurti is not easy to understand because the things he talks about are outside the range of ordinary comprehension. This is due to the fact that our minds are used to certain ways of thinking, whether we have orthodox or unorthodox views about life, and it is those accustomed ways of thinking which are the cause of all the trouble. They keep our thoughts along certain well-defined paths or ruts; and that makes our approach to, and understanding of, life and its problems so unsatisfactory. It is only when the mode of our thinking is fully understood in all its falsity that we can hope to adopt a way of living which is more satisfactory in the real sense, i.e., as bringing us more in touch with reality. It is the work of Krishnamurti to try to make us understand this fact and so enable us to break out of the moulds in which our minds are imprisoned. For that is the only way in which we can be set free; set free to gain a more sincere and direct appreciation of life, its meaning and significance.

Both Krishnamurti and Gurdjieff, two men vastly dissimilar in origin, upbringing and outlook, have the same motive in the line of work they initiated, although no doubt many sincere students would say there is really no apparent similarity between them. Superficially, this may seem to be so, but the writer thinks otherwise, and in the following pages will attempt to explain, and thereby—it is hoped—enable many people to contact a deeper and far more satisfying level of life and understanding than would be their lot otherwise. Gurdjieff is dead, and so are his co-worker Ouspensky, and the chief disciple of Ouspensky, Dr. Maurice Nicoll. It is in

the writings of Dr. Nicoll that we feel lies the bridge which
links the work of Gurdjieff with that of Krishnamurti;
especially in Dr. Nicoll's *Psychological Commentaries on the
Teachings of Gurdjieff and Ouspensky*. These Commentaries
comprise five volumes, and therein the student will find priceless *gems of wisdom*. These can introduce him to a deeper
level of living and of understanding *within himself*, and so
enable him to enter a world which is right outside that
in which we live ordinarily, yet it is the same world, but
contacted from an entirely different and far more spiritual
approach. The word spiritual is used in the sense of being
closer to *reality :* the reality of which the Universe itself is
made.

Through the Commentaries of Nicoll, and the teachings of
Krishnamurti, we feel that those who are seeking sincerely
for a more fundamental and truer mode of existence can find
the way thereto. When found it will be discovered to be
exactly the same way as that depicted by Christ in the
Gospels. This, of course, is as it should be. Christ himself,
and his teachings, are in full accord with the true spiritual
foundation of life and of the Universe. It is what orthodoxy
has made of them which has put so many people out of touch
with religious thought, and in opposition to what is claimed
to be Religion (but which obviously is not). Christ's teaching
about the Kingdom of Heaven is just as real today as it was
two thousand years ago, and his injunction to "Seek Ye first
the Kingdom of Heaven" is the key which can still unlock the
door to real spiritual progress and understanding.

It is our belief that in the Commentaries of Nicoll as in the
teachings of Krishnamurti we can again be shown the way to
tread again the very same path, and with identical results.
It means. however, a complete break with ordinary thinking;
it means *thinking in a new way :* in a way which people of
today do not understand. Therefore, we have to learn to think
in a new way if we are to achieve the salvation which really

satisfies our deepest instincts and brings us directly in touch
with REALITY.

To attempt to convey to readers some idea of the basic
requirements of such a quest, is the purpose of this book.
It is written by one who is primarily a student of Nicoll, and
only secondarily of Krishnamurti. He feels this fact should
be put on record, because he has found that the Commentaries
of Dr. Nicoll bridge the gap that exists between Krishnamurti
and his students, which Krishnamurti himself seems largely
unable to bridge.

The writer therefore hopes that in the following pages he
may be able to help others to discover the path to the real
understanding of themselves which he himself is trying to
tread, and which he feels is the key to the solution of the
whole problem of life which faces all of us.

CHAPTER I

MAN KNOW THYSELF

THROUGHOUT world history religion has always had its exoteric (external) and its esoteric (mysterious, secret) side. The religions of ancient Egypt, India, China, Greece, Judea, Persia, Arabia, etc., all conform to this twin tradition, because it is requisite of the human mind that there should be one type of religion for the masses, and another, more secret, type for those with the inner capacity to appreciate and understand it. It is not by accident that the inner teachings of all the known religions of antiquity are identical in essence, although in their externals they may differ very widely. The inner truths about the Universe and Man to be found in the religion of ancient Egypt are paralleled by those to be found in the Vedas, the ancient religious teachings of the Hindus; and in those of Buddhism, Taoism, Judaism, Hellenism, and, of course, Christianity. The esoteric teachings of Christianity have largely been lost from its exoteric aspect, but remain intact in the Gospels—for all those who have the eyes to see and the ears to hear—and it is a fact that Gurdjieff used to say that the system of inner development which he taught could be called esoteric Christianity. Its parallels with the Gospel teachings have been made even more clear by the work of the late Dr. Maurice Nicoll, especially in his books *The New Man* and *The Mark*.

The essence of this teaching can be summed up in the phrase chiselled over the portals of the ancient Greek temple

15

at Delphi: *Gnothi Seauton :* Know Thyself. It may seem
strange that only by knowing himself can man come to any
real understanding of the inner secrets and basic truths about
the Universe, but that is the case. Only when one really
understands what is implied by the phrase, Know Thyself, can
its immense importance and significance be realised.

Before man can know himself he must get used to the
idea that, at present, he does *not* know himself. The average
human being takes it for granted that he *does* know himself,
and would therefore assume that any further reference to the
subject is just a waste of time. Or, if he thought there was
anything at all in the injunction to know himself, he would
assume that everything required is covered by modern
psychology. He would take it for granted that in psychology
we have revealed to us the whole working of the inner
mechanism of man, i.e., *what makes him tick !*

Nothing could be further from the truth, and, indeed, that
is where lies the whole trouble with modern living. It is
because modern man does *not* know himself, but thinks he
does, and because modern psychology cannot reveal him to
himself, but thinks it can and does, that we have the present-
day problem of man being faced by the feelings—common to
all at times—of inner boredom, frustration, and futility, which
all try vainly to smother or ignore by the mass-excitements,
ambitions, and pursuits of present-day existence.

We make "getting on" our goal; we try to divert and amuse
ourselves with sport, radio, TV, the theatre, literature, etc.;
but deep down we know that we are *not* satisfied, and we
cannot understand the reason for our dissatisfaction. Some
think the answer is to be found in politics or economics—in
this or that ideology or creed, whether of the right or left;
some think the answer is to be found in the slogan : "back to
religion" (meaning orthodox religion in its many guises); some
think nothing matters, anyway, and that the best thing to do
is to try to forget about ourselves with the aid of drink, sex,

drugs, and so on and so forth. All are agreed, however, in their inmost hearts, if they are frank enough to face the fact, that life as lived today has something missing. What it is that is missing is something which no one seems to be able to discover.

We venture to assert that the only possible answer to the problem is to be found in the simple phrase we have already referred to : KNOW THYSELF. When man realises that at present he does *not* know himself, and that modern psychology cannot help him to know himself (because it deals only with his mental and emotional apparatus, and not with man as a totality, of which the mental and emotional apparatus is only a part), then we can possibly make a start in the right direction. It is precisely here that the works of both Gurdjieff and Krishnamurti come in. In their different ways they both set out to show man that at present he does not know himself, and they indicate the only way by which that self-knowledge is to be found.

Many have heard of the ancient Mystery Schools, whether of Egypt, Greece or elsewhere. The temple at Delphi, which bore over its portals the inscription we have quoted, conducted within its guarded precincts the teaching of The Mysteries (the inner realisation of what men were in themselves), and ancient Greek drama, which had its origins also in The Mysteries The dramas enacted in the temple, as part of the teaching of the neophyte, were concerned exclusively with the same theme. Externally, i.e., exoterically, Greek drama enacts the old legends and myths of the Greek religion, in the form of tragedy. But internally, i.e., esoterically, they really depict the struggle which goes on within the soul of man, wherein and whereby he gradually comes to a real understanding of himself, and eventually attains real emancipation from the darkness which veils the eyes and minds of mankind generally and keeps them prisoner to the follies and futilities which go to make up conventional living. It was the same in essence in the days of ancient Greece as it is today in modern Europe, America, or elsewhere.

Aeschylus, Sophocles, and that other great writer of Greek tragedy, Euripides, understood the real meaning and purpose of the dramas which they enacted. When one has the inner key one can see today exactly what they were trying to portray, just as one can in the more important plays of the immortal Shakespeare, when one understands their inner (esoteric) meaning. In fact, we can state categorically that all great drama is essentially concerned with the one theme of MAN, KNOW THYSELF, although externally and superficially there do not seem to be any grounds for so believing. When Oedipus all unknowingly marries his mother, after having—all unwittingly— slain his father, and later discovers what a terrible crime against the moral law he has committed, he wreaks an awful vengeance upon himself. This may seem merely like a grim tragedy with no other motive than to stir the blood and feelings of the audience; but to those who have the inner key it signifies something far more important in every way. It is all part of the inner development of man, stage by stage. The tragedy of Oedipus is merely the depiction, in dramatic and tragic form, of the process which can take place in the life of all of us, once our eyes are open to the need for self-awareness and self-knowledge as the only possible avenues towards the attainment of that real understanding of ourselves which Esotericism throughout the ages has proclaimed as the real destiny of evolving man. There are two forms of evolution: one is the mass-evolution which mankind as a whole takes part in without any real thought or understanding on his part; the other is that in which man engages *consciously,* because only through *it* can he develop the innate powers which are his by Divine right, i.e., his birthright as a human entity in the great Cosmic Plan of Creation.

The latter and more fundamental type of evolution is essentially *individual.* Mankind in general does not know of its existence, and must remain blindly unaware of it while pursuing aims and objectives which make its realisation an impossibility. But Esotericism has known the secret throughout the whole history of man, guarded in temple, mosque, and by the secret teachings of the Kabbalists, Alchemists, and seers and sages of all times. It is this very teaching which is now being put before the modern world in the works of Gurdjieff and Krishnamurti, albeit in their individual ways. It is all as old as the hills, yet it is still the newest thing ever; and it must always be so. It is the very old, but also the very new, because it is always new to those who have never encountered it before, yet it has always existed in the safe keeping of those who have been the custodians and guardians of the esoteric tradition.

Those who come across the teaching now for the first time can count themselves fortunate if they recognize its inherent value in terms of inner development, richness of life, and *purpose* in existence. The teaching supplies the only real purpose in living in a world wherein such purpose is entirely lacking, and which makes thinking men and women dissatisfied with life. Life without purpose is a sheer mockery and boredom, cover it up superficially as we may; life with purpose—real inner purpose—is the only kind of life worth living. It is only by obeying the injunction MAN, KNOW THYSELF that this hidden purpose is to be found.

It is no easy task, however; indeed, it demands the utmost endeavour and tenacity; but nothing could be more worthwhile and rewarding in its results. Once one has set one's feet upon the path of inner understanding and attainment, one begins to feel, at last, the beginning of a realization that we are all part of a wonderful world, and that man and the Universe are indeed one. Each one is part of THE ALL, and as such a part, a conscious part, a person becomes increasingly aware of that vast store of inner peace, beauty, and harmony which is the treasure that unfolds itself to man as a *conscious entity,*

in contradistinction to mass-mankind with its blind inability
to understand the need for self-knowledge, and its insensitive-
ness to all the wonders and miracles of the Universe which
Nature has showered upon us in such full measure.

CHAPTER II

THE WAY TO SELF-KNOWLEDGE

THE problem before modern man being to *know himself*, let us try to explain why it is that, at present, he does not do so. The reason for this lack of knowledge is because man believes that his person is all there is of him. He thinks that his physical body, with its mind and feelings, is the sum total of the entity which he feels himself to be. Some people—more materialistic—go so far as to deny that mind exists. But even those who are willing to concede that man has a mind distinct from his body, as well as emotions which are not purely the result of physical processes, have no idea where such "functions" of themselves may be located. Modern Psychology, whose province is the study of the mind and emotions, is equally unable to say what mind is or where it may be housed in the human entity. Nearly everyone seems to be agreed, however, that, whatever and wherever mind is, in the trinity of mind, emotions, and physical body we have all there is of man: *homo sapiens*. The more religious-minded aver that man has a soul and spirit, in addition to the other factors; but here again their location is a mystery. It is when we turn from Western Psychology to Eastern Psychology that we can begin to obtain an answer to our problem anent the basic constitution of man.

Many western people have no serious opinion about the knowledge and philosophy of the East. They probably assume with occidental self-assurance that whatever comes from the west must inevitably be superior to anything that may derive from the East. This is no doubt because in science and invention the Occident is so far ahead of the Orient. In matters of religion, philosophy and psychology, however, the East has a tradition of knowledge and under-standing which transcends anything known to Western minds, strange as this may seem.

In the ancient teachings of India, China, Egypt, etc., the inner truths relative to man's real constitution were fully known and taught to chosen disciples as part of the religious training of priesthood. It is only in comparatively recent years —less than a century—that this inner store of knowledge and wisdom has become available to the West, largely through the work of the late Madame H. P. Blavatsky, the founder of The Theosophical Society. The more one delves into this rich treasurehouse of knowledge and learning, the more is one astounded by its depth and profundity, and by its fore-shadowing—thousands of years ago—of many of the great discoveries of modern science. In these ancient scripts and teachings the knowledge of Evolution is to be found (an evolution more spiritual than anything known to modern science); also imparted were the facts about the atomic structure of matter, and the facts about the real construction of the stars and planets and universes with which modern astronomy is so much engrossed. All this, and much more, was known to the ancient sages and seers whose work comes down to us in the Vedas, and other holy writings of Eastern antiquity; and their knowledge of real psychology is astound-ing, too. They knew what man is *really* like, and solved the problem of the relationship between man's physical body, mind and emotions, by showing that there were other bodies possessed by the human entity, beyond the purely physical vehicle which we can all see.

The ancient Eastern teachings showed that there was an emotional body, composed of much finer matter than the physical, which interpenetrated the physical; and an even finer

THE WAY TO SELF-KNOWLEDGE

type of matter which constituted the mental body, which in
turn interpenetrated the emotional and physical bodies. Thus,
man has these interpenetrating bodies composed of ever-finer
material, which are blended together to form the composite
entity—man. Bodies even more evanescent go to form his soul
and spirit. In short, Eastern Psychology reveals man as having
seven interpenetrating bodies of varying densities of matter,
ranging from the most spiritual to the dense physical. It is this
seven-fold entity which man really is* although knowing only
of the purely physical in himself. Modern Science knows only
of the physical body and physical matter, although its
researches have made it realize that matter itself is only electricity in violent motion. Therefore, the invisible bodies we
have just referred to can be envisaged as imponderable forms
of cosmic electricity, which the methods and instruments of
present-day science are quite unable to perceive or contact.

Because of its knowledge of this sevenfold composition of
man, in various bodies of ever-finer matter, stretching down
from the most spiritual level to the coarse physical, and each
higher body interpenetrating all those lower than itself,
Eastern Psychology can help man to really understand
himself.

It is not essential for the purposes of this book for the
reader to accept the conception of the sevenfold constitution
of man in its entirety. He should be prepared, however, to
admit hypothetically that *it is possible* for man to be a much
more complex entity than he has been given cause to believe.
If we once admit the possibility of man being more than he
thinks superficially that he is, we can begin to show why the
current view of himself is unsatisfactory, and renders it
impossible for him to really know himself as he *really* is.

* Some systems number the interpenetrating bodies as five, whilst
the Gurdjieff system names four such bodies, i.e., physical, emotional,
mental and spiritual. But all such systems, which derive from the
Eastern tradition, have the same underlying principle, i.e., the inter-
penetration of bodies of ever-finer materiality.

If man thinks he is just a physical body with a mind and emotions incorporated somewhere and somehow, and—if orthodoxly religious-minded—believes he has also a soul and spirit in some form or guise entirely unknown, then man's gaze is centred more or less exclusively on that physical mechanism, with its mental and emotional attributes. He regards that as *himself*, and all his life is spent in trying to achieve as much satisfaction as possible—in terms of pleasure and the avoidance of pain—for the entity he considers to be himself.

The only world which modern man considers at all is the external world of which his senses make him cognizant. In other words, his whole life is *sense-based*, and everything he strives for or hopes for in the way of ambition, happiness, etc., comes to him via the senses. Even those who believe in the existence of soul and spirit, and an eternal life beyond the grave, still subscribe *in actuality*, if not in theory, with very few exceptions, to this self-same viewpoint. They *think* they believe in man as a spiritual being, but in actuality they behave generally as other people do, and have their centre of gravity in the physical body, mind, and emotions, with their senses as the key to conduct (i.e., the achievement of pleasure in its varied guises, and the avoidance of pain, discomfort, etc., insofar as personal circumstances, environment, etc., permit).

Looking at the matter dispassionately, it is easy to see that man's life today is ruled by the pleasure-pain principle. Through pleasure—whether crudely or more subtly manifested —man feels an expansion of himself (or what he regards as himself). Through pain—however manifested (i.e., whether mental, emotional or physical), he feels a depression or dimi-nution of himself. Thus his whole life swings between these two opposites which dominate him in every sphere of activity, whether to do with daily work, leisure, or anything else con-nected with his existence as an entity with the ability and power to think, feel and act.

If we call this trinity of physical body, mind and emotions *the self*, we can say that present-day man considers the self to be all that really exists of himself (apart from a purely hypothetical soul or spirit). Everything in his life is concerned with that self and how to make it more happy, comfortable, contented, etc., by whatever means he may consider available for the purpose. But it must also be conceded by clear-thinking people that far from man being able to achieve such objectives consistently, he is only able to do so fleetingly, and fitfully; while by far the larger part of his time is spent in bewailing the fact that he is unhappy, discontented, dejected, and fed-up with himself and with life generally.

In short, although man makes the attainment of pleasure and happiness his goal in living, he fails to achieve that objective, and only succeeds in achieving their opposite—interspersed here and there with a little pleasure and happiness and very unstable contentment. To live a life of real happiness and contentment is quite beyond his powers. He feels constantly that there *must* be some way in which this can be achieved, and so he is always looking around for means for this fulfilment. At one time he thinks he can achieve the happiness he desires through money, power, ambition satisfied, and so forth; at other times he thinks it is to be found in work for humanity in the social and political field; or in more aesthetic guise through literature, art, music, etc.; or by immersing himself in scientific work, philosophy, or religion. But if he still thinks that the self is the reality within him, and its satisfaction via the senses the sole criterion of successful living, no matter in what direction he may turn he is always and forever doomed to disappointment. Why? Because in looking to the self for real satisfaction and happiness in living, man is looking in entirely the wrong direction. He must look to something *beyond* the self, to something which is entirely beyond the physical gaze and not capable of being contacted

directly by the senses. He must look to that part of himself
composed of the more refined and spiritual portions of that
sevenfold structure which we have already said Eastern
Psychology reveals as the real fabric of man. The self which
we all know and take for granted is only the lower and coarser
aspects of this entity. It is the higher portions of it that form
what we may call the *REAL I or Individuality,* and the
activities of the ordinary self prevent this from being
manifested.

It is important not to identify this more interior Self with
the terms soul or spirit. This will only serve to confuse the
issue. The terms soul or spirit (as commonly understood) do
not apply here, because this Interior Self does not have to wait
for death and a life beyond the grave to manifest, it can
manifest here and now—at any time—so long as the opportunity is provided for it to do so.

That opportunity can only be forthcoming, however, when
we know of the existence of the Interior Self, and also realize
that it is the everyday self—which we regard as ourselves—
which is the chief stumbling-block in the way of the fundamental self emerging into ordinary life. In short, man
possesses two selves, not one, and the more fundamental and
truer self is not at all the same as the everyday self we know,
and can never manifest itself so long as we believe the
ordinary self is our only self. As long as we persist in thinking
so, so long will the more fundamental self be incapable of
making itself known to us and guiding our lives for us. It is
only when the fundamental self is allowed to manifest itself
and rule our lives that we can hope for real happiness and
contentment in living : the two things which the ordinary self
desires most, but is unable to secure for itself.

Hence the reason for the injunction carved over the portal
of the ancient Greek temple at Delphi: *GNOTHI SEAUTON:*
KNOW THYSELF. Until man does know himself for what
he really is, i.e., a self which is the compound of his physical

body, mind and emotions, and incorporates a fundamental Self which is the real centre and core of his being, he will continue to make mistakes and follies throughout his life. In regarding his ordinary self as all there is of him, he is considering the wrong part of himself for the achievement of whatever he deems best in living, and neglecting that which can really confer happiness and contentment upon him.

The happiness and contentment which the deeper and more fundamental Self makes possible is far different from the happiness and contentment which the everyday self is seeking; and this, of course, is where the rub comes in. Man seeks for happiness in the wrong way and through the wrong medium, and so must inevitably be frustrated, no matter what may be his walk in life, or his gifts and potentialities. He is doomed to failure from the start because he is going about things in the wrong way and for the wrong motives. Until he knows himself for what he really is, and can take steps to curb his everyday self, allowing his more fundamental and deeper Self to operate, his life will continue to be a burden and disappointment.

Fortunately, throughout all recorded history there have always been those who knew the truth of this statement; and, indeed, it is the central core of all true religious teaching, no matter what the religion. It is real *Esotericism,* which teaches the real meaning and purpose of life to man, and can show him the way to such attainment. As already indicated in this book, the same teaching is to be found in the writings of Maurice Nicoll and Krishnamurti, together with the key to the attainment of the goal itself. To be able to write about the subject is one thing, but to be able to point out the actual steps which have to be taken to achieve the objective of the quest is quite another thing. Indeed, the latter constitutes the most important individual training anyone, who realises for himself the desirability of such an aim, can undertake; and it is therefore beyond price. In the chapters which follow we shall try to point out the ways in which this realisation can be achieved; but naturally it is only by referring to the written works of Maurice Nicoll and Krishnamurti that the real practice can be followed. All we can do is to point the way. It is for those interested to apply in their own lives the ideas put forward through an assiduous study of those writings (as well as of Ouspensky's *In Search of the Miraculous*).

This path is indeed the only path to real self-knowledge, a knowledge which can transform the life of every man and woman who essays the task. It can lead them to the peace which passeth all understanding, because it brings them into direct communion with the more fundamental portion of themselves which they never knew existed. It is truly the *divine* part of themselves, because it is rooted in the same Creative Essence which created the external universe in which we live and move and have our being!

CHAPTER III

IMAGINARY "I"

IN the previous chapter we indicated that the human entity can be divided into two parts : the ordinary self (personality), and the more real but invisible part of himself (individuality). All of us consider the personality to be ourselves, and assume that it is one consistent entity. This is quite an illusory idea, and is the source of countless difficulties in everyday living. Apart from the fact that the personality is not our real Self, it is neither a definite self nor entity. It is one thing one minute, and quite another thing the next, according to which idea or attitude within us is dominant at the time. At one moment we may be immersed in eating, shall we say, but the next minute we may be involved in an argument about politics with someone with whom we may happen to be having lunch. The "I" in us which is immersed in eating is not the same "I" which is engaged in a discussion about politics, although both "I's" are housed in the same physical body and use the same mental and emotional mechanism through which to express themselves.

This is a very difficult idea to grasp properly. It should not be pushed aside as absurd. It is far from absurd, and, once grasped, the idea can make a vast difference to our understanding of ourselves and of other people, too. We are all exactly alike in this respect. We are full of thousands of these various "I's", each of which embodies some idea or attitude or viewpoint, some of the "I's" being far more powerful and long-standing than others, and some being quite weak and

29

recent. But, once we are awake to the situation and begin to watch ourselves, it is quite easy to see in ourselves the various "I's" at work, one taking the place of another in rapid succession during the day. This happens according to the situation or circumstances involved through the embodiment of ideas, wishes, beliefs—in short all the paraphernalia of the thought and emotional life of the personality resulting from upbringing, education, social factors, and the moulding influences of life generally.

Therefore, according to the Gurdjieff system, what we call *ourselves* is just an imaginary entity, or an illusion. It just does not exist, although to ourselves and everyone else it seems quite real and indeed solid. It is given illusory steadfast continuity merely because of the fact that it is the same physical body which is being utilised all the time, and the same mind and emotions.

Once this seemingly obscure and strange idea has been grasped properly, why we behave so differently at different times and under different situations will be made clear. At one moment we are carefree and happy, and in the next something may plunge us into the deepest gloom, while immediately after this we may perhaps find ourselves just bored or indifferent about everything. This is all according to which "I" has been stimulated into activity by the circumstances of the day. Of course, it is embarrassing and humiliating to have to admit that we are not one real and compact entity all the time; it is a blow to our pride in ourselves; and many people may never get to the point where they are ready to make this admission. But for those who can see its truth, it will pave the way for the first attempt to really know and understand themselves, which is the sole purpose of esoteric teaching and training.

This knowledge that we are simply a mass of conflicting "I's" brought into existence through upbringing, education, social factors, suggestion, literature, radio, TV, and all the other factors to which we are exposed and which mould our thoughts and feelings, makes us realise that the "I" we consider ourselves to be—Mr. A., Miss B., etc.—is merely the product of imagination: *our imagination about ourselves*. It is only when we can understand this vital fact and can set to work to develop the more real part of ourselves—hitherto unknown and never thought about—that we can hope eventually to become a real entity. This entity will be *consistent* within itself, because it is ruled from within by *consciousness*, and is not the plaything of the hour that we are today, ruled by external factors and lack of knowledge about our true position in regard to ourselves.

Thus, there is a great difference between the self that we are at present, and that which we may some day become as a result of working upon ourselves in the manner and under the conditions which esoteric training will command. Then we shall understand why it is we may say something one day and do something quite the opposite the next; why we make promises or resolves of various kinds which we do not keep; why we are constantly doing things we really do not want to do and are ashamed of ourselves for doing, etc. We do all these things yet retain the illusion that despite them we are one complete and always-the-same entity, because our name happens to be Mr. So-and-So who lives at such-and-such an address. Never for one moment do we realise that we are nothing of the sort. It is exactly the same with everyone else, of course.

How frequently are we perplexed by seeing people doing or saying things which are immediately contradicted by what they do or say next? We fail to understand such conduct in others, and think *we* would never do those things. But, of course, we do exactly the same, only we never notice that we do so. We see these things in others but never in ourselves, because it is all part of the gigantic illusion in which we are all engulfed that makes us see ourselves as conscious beings always knowing what we are doing and always being quite sure we are the same person all the time, no matter what the amazing vagaries of our conduct may be. Others see the vagaries, just as we see the vagaries of their conduct, but we never see our *own* vagaries, because of the blindness and false ideas about ourselves with which we are beset.

Hence, the first purpose of the Gurdjieff system is to make people *aware* that the "I" they always think themselves to be is merely imaginary, which, in Gurdjieff's system is known as "IMAGINARY 'I'". Once we are really aware of this fundamentally important fact, our whole attitude to ourselves will begin to change. Unless and until we change our attitude to ourselves, there is no possibility of starting to acquire that self-knowledge which is the basic factor in the transformation of ourselves from imaginary people into real people, with something stable and solid within our lives, which is the result of conscious and consistent work on ourselves.

Krishnamurti does not approach this particular subject in exactly the same way, although fundamentally he works in the same direction by trying to make us realise the essential falseness and illusoriness of the personality, with its many shifts and changes according to the predominant idea of the moment which dominates that entity which we call ourselves.

Modern Psychology is concerned essentially and only with the personality or everyday self—the Illusory or Imaginary "I". It is this illusory "I" which conventional psychology regards as constituting our "self", just as we all do. The work of psychologists is concerned entirely with the problems of the imaginary self, which they, too, take to be entirely consistent and always the same. When Mr. A. is in need of psychological advice, the psychologist regards him as one entire person, not a conglomeration of conflicting persons, as the man is; and so he tries to sort out their difficulties and problems while working under this delusion. We need not wonder, therefore, why so much of present-day psychological work is lacking in success. It may succeed temporarily, in certain cases, and more so with some people than with others. As, however, the psychologist's problems are identical with those of his patients, because he, too, takes himself for one complete entity, whereas he is only a confused mass of conflicting "I's" all jockeying for position and pushing him this way and that quite often against his will, and without his being in the least aware of the fact : we need not be surprised that psychological disorders are fast increasing in all civilised countries.

We are all in the same boat, psychologists and all, and continue our day-to-day existence entirely under the sway of our Imaginary "I". It is useless to look to conventional psychology for any solution of our basic problems in living, because psychologists need just as much attention as we do. They may be able to help the unbalanced and mentally unstable to become somewhat more balanced and stable, we admit. Those who are supposed to be already balanced and stable they cannot help at all, because their troubles are right outside the psychologist's province, and affect each and every one of us (himself included).

It is interesting to note, in this connection, that Dr. Nicoll was himself a noted psychologist, and studied under Jung in Zurich. He gave up his practice eventually to teach the system he was taught by Gurdjieff and Ouspensky, which is called THE WORK, because he realised that only through that system, which is sometimes termed *Esoteric Psychology*, could man really transform himself from the unreal being he now is (although not aware of the fact) into the real entity he could become, through consistent work on himself, via the teachings of THE WORK.

We repeat : the first essential is to change one's attitude to oneself, to regard oneself differently; not as one always has done hitherto. The teaching about the Imaginary "I" is the first essential to be grasped if we wish to tread the path of

Self-knowledge and Self-awakening which is the purpose of our quest into the realms of Esotericism. There are many different systems in existence which are termed esoteric, but nothing can be really genuine which begins with man as he is and tries to work on him from that level. Man must leave his present state of non-awareness about himself to become aware of himself, as part of the process of Self-knowledge, and that is why this teaching about the Imaginary "I" is vitally important. It marks the first step on the path towards the real understanding of ourselves which is the only thing that can help us to solve our present-day problems in living, and eventually become really conscious entities with a real core or centre within us which is our REAL SELF.

CHAPTER IV

SELF-OBSERVATION

[handwritten: 1 step which leads to Self Knowledge]

HAVING made the reader aware of the Imaginary "I" in himself, the next step is to make him verify this fact through an examination of himself during his day-to-day activities. Unless he can really see that he is merely a mass of conflicting and contradictory "I's", he will never be in a position to begin to work on himself in order to become a *real* being. For this purpose the Gurdjieff system uses a technique known as *Self-observation*. We have to *observe ourselves*, in short. This is far from being as simple as it sounds. To begin with, most people take it for granted that they do observe themselves, merely because they are aware of what they may be doing or saying, and so on. That sort of thing is not *real* self-observation. To be able to observe oneself, in the sense we mean, one must be able to divide oneself into two, as it were, so that "something" within one is able to observe what the rest of the personality is doing. One has to bring into existence a latent power capable of doing this. Everyone has that latent power within him, although most of us never make use of it throughout our lives. This ability to detail a certain portion of ourselves to watch or observe what the rest of us is doing or saying, is the first practical step towards our goal of self-knowledge. Until we can actually see what the personality is doing (i.e., actually become consciously aware of the fact), we shall continue doing the wrong things we did previously.

Self-observation serves more than one purpose in our task

of acquiring self-knowledge. It makes it clear to us that we are *not* one consistent always-the-same person, and—more important still—it also makes it clear that our daily activities are merely *reactions* towards events, rather than actual conscious and purposive actions of our own volition. This, indeed, is something which the average person will at first flatly deny. We all do so when the idea is first put to us. But, after a time, and as a result of careful self-observation, we are forced to admit that this is really so. It is quite a blow to our pride to have to admit it; but unless we are absolutely honest with ourselves we cannot possibly succeed in our quest. Thus we are forced to accept the fact—as a result of sincere self-observation—that we *never* act in relation to events in our lives, but only *react*. It *seems* as though we are acting purposively, but it is exactly the same thing as the Imaginary "I". The whole thing is just a gigantic illusion.

For instance, when we rise up in the morning, and it is a fine day, we feel pleased. If it is raining or snowing, we feel displeased, and start the day feeling moody and depressed. Then, when we go down to breakfast, and it is not to our liking, here is something else we react to by feeling disgruntled; or, if to our liking, we may feel that it is not such a bad morning after all ! Then, if we have some post, and open a letter bringing good news, we begin to think that this is quite a nice world to live in, despite its many drawbacks. Conversely, if previously we had been feeling pleased with ourselves, and then opened a letter bringing bad news, all our pleasure would disappear in a flash and we would be plunged into gloom. And so on and on right through the day. From morning to night our whole life is one round of reacting to the events which are presented to us through our social position, work, personal interests of all kinds, world events, and everything else that goes to make up our environment.

We may regard ourselves as a focal point towards which events of all kinds, from all parts of the compass, send out shafts which strike the centre which is ourselves, causing us to react this way and that, in accordance with our mental and emotional equipment. Naturally, the mental and emotional equipment of people differs one from another, according to upbringing, education, home life, etc. That is why we all react to events differently, although it is *all* reacting. It may seem like conscious activity on our part, but as self-observation will show, it is merely reaction, being our purely mechanical response to the situation of the moment. According to our make-up so will be our reaction. That is another vitally important fact about ourselves which the Gurdjieff system makes clear; and in his talks and writings Krishnamurti enunciates the same truth in his own particular way.

To realise the fact that we merely react to events, and are purely mechanical beings may hurt our pride very much, but the process of self-knowledge *must* hurt, otherwise we cannot change ourselves from what we are at present into the beings we have to become.

The conception about reacting mechanically to events is not a purely materialistic one, as it may seem at first sight. There are materialistic philosophies which postulate the idea that man is a mere mechanism and has his whole life determined for him by external events. According to such philosophies there is no possibility of changing the situation. Man is born a mechanism and remains one until the end of his days. According to the teachings we are discussing, however, the situation is quite different. It is expressly stated that man *can* change from the mechanical being he is now, into a really conscious entity who is in charge of his own life, instead of life being in charge of him, as it were. Thus the two ideas are diametrically opposed, although seeming to resemble one another at first glance.

Therefore, through self-observation we are made to realise our own mechanicalness, our mere reaction to the events of daily life, and the fact that instead of being one consistent and complete entity, we are merely a mass of conflicting and mutually warring "I's". This is quite a lot, indeed, for any individual to accept; but, unless one is prepared to do so, it is quite impossible to gain that understanding of ourselves which *THE WORK* demands. Another fundamental teaching of The Work used in connection with what we are discussing is that *man is asleep,* and the purpose of The Work is to wake him up. Quaintly enough, man is asleep as long as he regards himself as a fully conscious being, in full control of his life. He can only begin to wake up when—through careful self-observation—he becomes aware of the various facts we have touched on in the present chapter. In this context self-observation must always be *uncritical.* It is no use trying to observe ourselves if we are going to criticise what we may consider to be wrong, and praise what we may consider to be right. That leads only to *identification,* which is another of the important factors in our make-up which leads to so much trouble in our lives. Indeed, we may perhaps say that identifying is our greatest curse. It is the greatest of all stumbling-blocks to inner development. Esoteric Psychology sets out to make us aware of it, and then gradually to try to overcome it. If and when we can overcome the habit of identifying, which is our common failing, then, indeed, we will have taken a really great stride forward in our task of self-knowledge and self-unfoldment.

In the system we are discussing, *to identify* means *to become one with* whatever it may happen to be that we identify with. For instance, if we are upset over something we unconsciously identify with that feeling of being upset; we say *we* are upset. That means we put ourselves completely into the feeling in question; at the moment it occurs, that feeling is *us.* And exactly the same with everything else that happens in our lives. Whatever it may be, pleasure, discomfort, boredom, frustration, delight, we identify completely with it all, and lose ourselves in the feeling or thought or action, whatever it

may happen to be. From our present standpoint this is exactly
as it should be, and shows how terribly difficult it is to make
people see what Esoteric Psychology is trying to show them.
Ordinary psychology takes identifying for granted as something which is quite natural and right; and from its standpoint
it is quite right in doing so. Every psychologist does exactly
the same thing himself, and sees nothing wrong in it. To him
it is the *natural* thing to do. And so it is, at the present level
(the level at which we all are at present). That is why it is so
necessary to understand the mechanism of identification, so as
to be able to recognize it in ourselves, through self-observation,
in order to be able to get to a point where we can begin
not to identify. Once we reach that stage we begin to dis-
sociate our real self from the false self (or personality) which
always identifies with everything, and considers it as quite the
normal and natural thing to do. (We must emphasize that the
term Identification as used in ordinary psychology is not at
all the same thing. It has a quite different and very limited
significance).

Having explained very briefly *why* we have to observe ourselves, and the light it throws on our psychological mechanism,
the reader may be pardoned for thinking that it is exactly the
same thing as introspection. But this is quite wrong. When
we are introspective we are completely immersed in ourself
(in the ordinary everyday self or personality). We are, then,
also completely identified, of course. But when we carry out
self-observation properly we begin to *separate* from ourself
(from the ordinary everyday self) because we watch what that
everyday self is doing, and mentally note its antics. Therefore,
introspection and self-observation are diametrically opposed
in action and effect, and should never be confused one with
another. In the teachings of Krishnamurti the process of self-
observation, without criticism, is called *watching,* or *passive
self-awareness.* It is the only method whereby we may become
really conscious of ourself in our everyday thoughts, feelings

and actions, and no system which does not employ it can be called really esoteric.

There are many systems which purport to make us into different beings; which will help us to get on in life; become more "successful" maybe; more "spiritual" perhaps, etc., all according to the type of system and what its aims are. But any system purporting to be esoteric which does not employ the technique of self-observation or passive self-awareness, is unable to help us towards real self-knowledge, because it is not supplying us with the first and most essential implement for our task. We can never begin to know ourselves without self-observation, as already emphasized, and it is only through self-knowledge that any real inner development is possible. To become what he may be, man must change from what he is. That is self-evident. Until he can really see what he is at present, he will never come to realize the need for changing himself. Therefore self-observation is an essential prerequisite for his task. Without it he cannot progress. In the *Psychological Commentaries* of Dr. Nicoll self-observation is explained in great detail from a wide variety of angles. With this invaluable aid the neophyte can begin to really work on himself towards the end of ultimate self-knowledge, which term is synonymous with real inner self-development (i.e., the discovery and bringing into full activity of the real Self within, in contradistinction to the everyday self which we now think is our real Self, but which is nothing of the sort.)

The reader should by now be beginning to see how vastly different Esoteric Psychology is from ordinary psychology, and why only the former can help us in the task we have in hand.

CHAPTER V

SELF-REMEMBERING

IN the previous chapter we indicated that self-change is essential, if we are to make any headway with the esoteric system we are discussing. We showed that self-observation is the first prerequisite in effecting this change in one's attitude to oneself. One has to begin to view oneself entirely differently from the way one has considered oneself heretofore. The old self which one has always assumed oneself to be has to be allowed to fall gradually into the background, and an entirely different Self has to be allowed to emerge into the foreground, as it were. But first, of course, this new Self (which is really a very old Self, but hitherto quite unknown, because submerged by the personality which we have regarded as ourself) will be a complete stranger to us. *Then how can we begin to become aware of it?* This may be effected by a technique known as *Self-Remembering.* The Self is denoted by a capital S to distinguish it from the ordinary self, or personality. Throughout the whole teaching of the Gurdjieff system constant emphasis is laid on the need to *Self-Remember, or Remember Ourselves.* In the ordinary course of everyday living we are immersed completely in the personality. We are identified with its actions, wishes, thoughts, desires, etc., and are therefore totally ignorant of the existence of the other and deeper Self, which Self-Remembering will bring to our attention. Therefore, the act of Self-Remembering has been especially designed to break the complete sway of the personality, and to make us aware—if only for brief flashes of time—of the existence of something far greater and deeper within us.

The idea behind Self-Remembering, therefore, is to try to instil within us a conscious awareness of the existence of something far greater and nobler than the everyday self. It brings us into touch with levels of ourself untouched hitherto, and so it has a profound esoteric significance. We are exhorted to Remember Ourselves as often as possible every day, so as to bestir ourselves from that state of sleep in which we usually live.

But remembering ourselves has other values besides the one just mentioned. We do not have to try to remember ourselves in a vacuum, as it were. The idea is to try to remember ourselves at moments during the day when we are more than ordinarily involved in the troubles and difficulties which constantly beset and harass the personality. (That is to say, when we are most identified with the personality and its particular problems.) If we can do this not only do we attain momentarily a higher level of ourselves, we also tend to break the hold of the personality for that particular instant, just when its power seems at its most potent. The reader will no doubt appreciate the significance of this statement. If he does it will help to show him how tremendously important the act of Self-Remembering is and can be.

Further, by constantly trying to recall this more deep-seated and vastly more important Self to our minds, we set up currents which make it increasingly easier for us to become consciously aware of it. We begin to have "flashes" of its presence within us.

The technique of Self-Remembering has, therefore, a most important part to play in the esoteric system under discussion. In Dr. Nicoll's *Commentaries* its many and varied aspects are touched on in all sorts of different ways and from different viewpoints, thus making us aware of the many-sided nature of the conception, and of its deep importance to the student.

The best way to gain a picture of the subject is as follows : we can think of ourselves being swept along in the current of daily life, with all kinds of troubles and difficulties constantly facing the harassed personality; and there beyond—outside of it all, clothed in its own inherent divinity—is this REAL SELF which is *really* US, calm and serene. It is waiting for us to contact IT and so partake of ITS greatness in so far as we are able to keep ITS existence in our minds for that particular occasion. The more frequent the occasions, the more will we tend to partake of that REAL SELF'S majesty and divinity, and be affected by IT in our day-to-day life, which will be gradually and increasingly transformed from what it is at present. That life, lived under the stresses and strains of modern civilisation via the aegis of the personality, with its wishes, desires, ambitions, lusts, selfishnesses, etc., will be made different in every way, so that in time we shall become completely changed beings.

Of course, that is only one aspect of the system of esoteric training and development which we are discussing. It fits in with all the other aspects, as each has its particular rôle or part to play in the total design. In certain respects, however, it is the most fundamental aspect of all, bringing us into direct contact with the deepest and grandest levels of OURSELF (our *REAL SELF*).

In The Work terminology, everything connected with the act of Self-Remembering, in all its varied aspects, is called "giving oneself the first conscious shock". By the term "first conscious shock" is meant a deliberate act of will, consciously entered into by the student, with full knowledge of what it is intended to achieve. It is intended to wake us up from the hitherto sleeping state in which we have lived under the full sway of the personality. Anything that can do this for us is a shock (in The Work terms), and it is only through these shocks that we can grow more conscious as time goes on. By such a gradual increase in consciousness we can bring about the progressive transformation of ourselves which is the objective of the system we are discussing. By administering to ourselves the first conscious shock, we are told that we introduce finer energies into our system, which tend to create the higher forms of matter which are required before our higher centres can operate. The higher centres are dormant when we live our lives exclusively within the narrow confines of the personality. Such teachings are very recondite and need considerable study to understand fully. We merely mention them here, in passing, to show the reader how deep and detailed is the whole system. As indicated in the Preface, we are concerned only in introducing the subject to the reader. If he or she has by this time become really interested, the means for further and more detailed study is provided by the information supplied in later pages.

In the next chapter we shall deal with a subject almost as important in its way as Self-Remembering, but in sharp contradistinction to it; namely *self-justifying,* which in many ways may be regarded as the besetting sin of our age.

CHAPTER VI

SELF-JUSTIFYING

ONE weakness that is common to mankind is the practice of self-justifying. Whatever we may do that seems wrong or unjust in other people's eyes, in our own we are always right. We can always adduce adequate reasons for whatever we may have done or said. Such reasons may not—and often do not —satisfy other people, especially those who may feel wronged or hurt by our acts or words; but they do satisfy *us,* and as far as we are concerned that is all that really matters. The whole process is what we mean here by the expression *self-justifying.* Through it we preserve our own feeling of "always being right" which is precious to our self-esteem. It is all done so unconsciously that it often requires diligent self-observation to make us aware of the extent to which we do self-justify. In fact, it may be regarded as an automatic reaction. It is all part of that mechanical and automatic reaction to the events of life which Esoteric Psychology terms sleep. Man is fast asleep within himself, snugly assuming that he is a fully conscious being, aware of all that he is doing, and initiating activity in everything he undertakes—whereas he is merely a mechanism blindly reacting to every situation and event that confronts him. Of all the mechanisms which sustain him in that feeling of smug self-satisfaction with himself, the chief one is self-justifying. Through its automatic use in his life man goes on living, feeling quite certain within himself that whatever he does or says or thinks is right, however much other people may contradict him. But they, too, self-justify, and so it is an unending process in which we are all involved, everyone self-justifying, and seeing where others may be wrong, but never really seeing what may be wrong in what they may be saying or doing.

When we begin to apply self-observation, however, we can realise self-justifying at work, and then try to take steps to stop its insidious work. The obvious purpose of self-justifying is to bolster up our own pride and belief in ourselves, which are essential to our morale, the morale of the personality which we think we are. When that morale is destroyed or even unduly disturbed, we feel inevitably that our whole identity is being threatened. That is something which the personality can never withstand. Hence the blind automatism of the mechanism of self-justifying. It is a mental process which is so much part of ourselves that it may almost be called instinctive.

It is not part of the *instinctive* nature of man to self-justify, because if we lived in the *real* part of ourselves we would never self-justify. There would be no need for it. Self-justifying belongs only to the unreal part of ourselves, the personality. At a very early age children learn to self-justify, because they learn it from their elders who are continuously doing it. Self-justifying is not something which is innate to the mental and emotional mechanism of man. It is a purely artificial thing which has been implanted in our thinking apparatus, as it were, because of the essential falseness of the personality it is always being called upon to defend. If self-justifying could be eradicated from adult humanity, children coming into the world would not self-justify as soon as they were able to talk; it would be something quite foreign to their natures. Which only goes to show how utterly warped are our natures, as the result of living completely in the wrong part of ourselves.

When one has carried out self-observation over a long period one begins to appreciate how deep-seated and auto-

matic self-justifying is, and how terribly difficult it is to
eradicate. It is widely prevalent for people to say automatically : "It wasn't my fault", "I couldn't help it", etc.,
when anything happens in which they may happen to be
involved. Many people say it even if they know it *was* really
their fault, but they all too rarely bring themselves to own up
to the fact. The usual reaction is to try to blame it on to
someone else, or on to circumstances outside one's control.
The whole process of self-justifying applies to matters not
only of merely superficial importance, but to the most important affairs and feelings of life. Always we try to justify whatever we do, because we cannot bear to think that anything we
have done can be really wrong, even though we may know
that it appears wrong to others. There is always the desire
within us to *see ourselves in the right*. This is something which
causes untold harm to our real inner unfoldment. Indeed,
there can be no attempt at inner unfoldment while we keep
up the habit of self-justifying, and that is why it is vitally
important to become aware of its existence, as part of our
training in Esoteric Psychology.

We must become completely aware of the extent and
insidiousness with which we self-justify, in order to stop self-
justification, for only when we do not self-justify can we start
to see ourselves as we really are, stripped of all pretence. We
pretend to ourselves all the time, in all sorts of ways, because
something in us demands that we do this; and that something
is the false self which we think we are. It can only keep in
command of us, it can only keep us in its thrall, so long
as we imagine it is our true self. That is why our false self
must self-justify over everything. It *has* to keep itself in
countenance. It just cannot live without an entirely illusory
sense of its own value, because it has no *real value* in itself,
and basically it knows that. Hence its frantic strivings to keep
us within its grip; and, as just made clear, we hope, self-
justifying is one of the chief agencies employed for its purpose.

When we do become aware of the appalling extent to which we self-justify, and can see what real harm it is doing to our true nature, we can begin to try to stop the process and accept the blame for whatever it is we may have said or done wrong. It is something which takes courage. It may be difficult to admit to others that we may have done this or that wrong; but the really difficult thing is to admit it *to ourselves*. That is by far the hardest task. For even when, perhaps, we have admitted to others that we may have done something or said something wrong, we still may find it terribly hard to admit it to ourselves, for we can always find reasons for self-justifying. In fact, there are no limits to which the ability to self-justify does not go in our personal lives. Being able to face up to ourselves fairly and squarely and admit, without equivocation of any kind, that what we may have been doing is *really wrong*, is a great step forward in self-knowledge, and a milestone upon our path to *real* Selfhood. The real Self never self-justifies; it has no need to do so.

Esoteric Psychology thus helps us to forge another link in the chain of self-revelation which is going to make us more and more aware of ourselves. We shall know ourselves to be unreal, and thereby make it possible for the Reality within us to be recognized and acclaimed. Until it is recognized and acclaimed we are really nothing; we are simply travesties of ourselves masquerading as people, merely because we have physical bodies and a mental and emotional equipment ready for our use. Before the self within us can be recognized and acclaimed, we have to become aware of the fact that *it actually exists*. If we do not know it exists, we cannot take any steps towards its recognition. Thus it is an essential prerequisite of Esoteric Psychology (or THE WORK) to make us aware that this basic or real Self does exist, ready to take over as soon as we make it possible for it to do so. That possibility can only arise when the personality is made *passive*, as it is termed in The Work phraseology.

At present it is the personality which is *active :* it is that part of ourselves of which we are aware and through which we think we *can do* (another Work phrase). But as a matter of fact *we cannot do,* in the sense of being able to initiate real activity in our present state. We react only to events, as indicated in a previous chapter. Therefore, before something more real can become active, personality has to begin to become passive. Through *self-observation,* and noting and watching *self-justifying* and trying not to *self-justify* or *identify,* we shall be taking big steps towards making the personality passive, the essential prerequisite for the emergence of *REAL I.*

The reader will observe how all the various aspects of work on oneself are linked up in the Gurdjieff system. Although he does not employ the same terms, Krishnamurti is working towards the same end by the methods he talks and writes about. He, too, wishes us to be liberated from our false self, so that what is *real* can take possession of our lives.

There is one factor we have not touched on, so far, in talking about personality and REAL I, and which is really the essential link between them, and that is what is known in Work terms as *essence.* Essence is the link between Personality and REAL I, because, as personality is made passive through work on oneself, essence becomes increasingly active in its place; and it is only when essence is completely active and supersedes personality that REAL I can take full command. We propose to deal with this subject in the following chapter. It is vitally germane to our whole theme.

CHAPTER VII

PERSONALITY AND ESSENCE

IN the present chapter we come to one of the most important teachings in Esoteric Psychology. We have made it clear that the individual we know as ourselves is merely the personality —the outer husk as it were—and not the real self, which remains unknown throughout life unless one learns about its existence through esoteric study and training. The personality itself can be divided into two parts: *false personality* and *personality proper*. According to the Gurdjieff system false personality is by far the larger portion of what we regard as our personality, being made up of all those elements which go to swell our ego, such as pride, vanity, self-conceit, imaginations and day-dreams about ourselves, etc.; whereas personality proper is that part of personality which has been developed during life through education, vocation, training and study of all kinds, etc. In short, personality proper is the part of personality which is of real value in earning our living, and making us acquainted with the "know how" of existence. It contains within it all aptitudes, abilities, and prowesses which we may have acquired or developed through life. It is therefore something of *real value* although not part of the real self of man. False personality, on the other hand, that part of personality within which we mostly live, is of no real value to us. During esoteric training false personality is essentially that part which must be weakened if we are to make any true headway towards becoming *real people*. In other words, false personality is our greatest enemy; it is the enemy lurking forever within us ready to destroy and devour us.

What about essence? We were born with what The Work calls *essence,* which may be regarded as an expression of our own true nature *(of what we really are).* As soon as we are born personality begins to develop as a result of upbringing, training, education, imitation of older people, etc., but there is no corresponding growth of essence. Essence remains in its infantile state, whilst the human entity grows. It may remain in that infantile state throughout life, even though the person may become quite famous in whatever field (or fields) of activity they may spend their lives. In short, there is no corresponding growth between personality and essence. The more that false personality develops as an accretion around personality itself, the less possibility can there be for any growth of essence. Our true essential nature thus becomes completely overlaid by false personality, and this is so with by far the vast majority of people throughout the civilized world.

More primitive types of people, in whom false personality is not very much developed, can have a certain growth of essence, and so can people who live close to Nature, or do creative work with their hands, and so on. In such people essence has a certain amount of opportunity for growth, but it is strictly limited. It is only when—as a result of esoteric training—we really understand what is here involved, that we can begin to take the importance and emphasis out of personality (and especially false personality), and transfer the importance and emphasis to the building up and development of essence. In other words, in The Work terminology we have to seek to make personality *passive* (instead of active as heretofore) and essence *active* (instead of allowing it to remain passive as previously). In short, essence has to be allowed to feed on personality, and grow at its expense, thereby making it possible for REAL I to come into evidence more and more

fully in our lives. The REAL I can do this only when essence
is more fully developed as a result of our work on ourselves
in making personality increasingly passive (through non-
identifying, non-self-justifying, and so on). In the process false
personality has to be made gradually weaker and weaker.
That part of ourselves is no good at all, and must be eradicated; but the best features of real personality can be used
by essence in its own growth and development as skills and
abilities through which it can express itself.

For instance, let us consider an egg. There is the yolk, the
white and the shell. If we regard false personality as the outer
hard shell, and personality as the white, then we can see that
for the yolk (essence) to develop into a bird it has to feed on
the white (personality) and ultimately the bird has to break
through (destroy) the shell before it can emerge fully into the
light of day as a living creature. That is exactly what has to
happen with us if we wish to become really living men and
women instead of the travesties of such which we really are,
no matter how seemingly important and successful we may be
in the eyes of the world and of ourselves. In the Gurdjieff
system the means whereby the personality can be acted upon
and rendered more passive so as to enable essence to grow
and become the vehicle for the ever-fuller expression of
REAL I, are made very clear. A study of Dr. Nicoll's
Commentaries is richly rewarding in this respect. Here, we
can but point the way to the reader. We are attempting to
show him the need for such an attitude to himself as is
depicted in the relationship between personality and essence
that is briefly described in the present chapter. For his real
self to grow, his present personality (composed so largely of
false personality) *must be diminished.* That is the operative
phrase, and once the reader has grasped the reason for this,
then he will be ready to make a more detailed and serious
study of the subject, and the means whereby the process can
be attempted.

In regard to the question of personality it is important to point out that in the Gurdjieff system great stress is laid upon the fact that before one is ready to come into The Work one must be at the stage of what is known as *good householder*. That is to say, one must be in the position where one is able to earn one's livelihood competently, thereby showing that one is able to cope reasonably successfully with the problems of everyday existence and to accept full responsibility for the discharge of one's obligations. One who is a failure in ordinary living is not regarded as one ready to take up The Work, because until one has shown some mastery over external affairs it is not regarded as likely that he would be able to develop any mastery over himself and his internal affairs. That view is in sharp contradistinction to the views held by many esoteric systems, which often say (or seem to say) that the more one is unable to stand up to ordinary life the better chance is there for real esoteric development (such development being regarded as utterly divorced from ordinary living). The system we are dealing with, however, does not subscribe at all to that viewpoint. It lays down categorically the idea of *good householder* as the basic requirement for the task of esoteric development or training, and we feel ourselves that it has every right to do so. Linked up with The Work teaching about good householder, is also another teaching about the existence of what is called Magnetic Centre, which is referred to more fully later in this chapter.

Far too many people who are failures in life seek to turn to more idealistic modes of living or thinking as an escape from their failure. They have found life too much for them and think they can find a more easy route through non-material sources of living. But this method is never a success in terms of real inner development, however successful it may appear to be as a mode of escapism. For escapism and true esotericism are poles apart, as anyone can see who tries to get to grips with himself through the medium of The Work.

It demands the sternest reality to oneself, and escapism has no room for itself in such a process.

The fact that one must be a good householder before one is ready to attempt the Gurdjieff system rules out very young people from the attempt. This is precisely as it should be. Before one can work on personality (and especially false personality) there must have been many years of growth for these features of ourselves; and very young people have not had the time so to develop themselves. They are still in the embryo stage, as it were, with regard to personality development. Not that we regard personality development as a good thing *per se*, although the better part of personality has its value, as we have attempted to show. Essence can only grow at *the expense* of personality, so that if there is no personality developed there is not much scope for essence to develop either. This is a very important point of the teaching to bear in mind.

Another important point is this : many people who are attracted to The Work think they can add it to their personalities. They think they can take themselves as they are now, and, through work on themselves, become esoterically developed. That is quite impossible. The essence of esotericism is that we have to *change ourselves*, i.e., become different beings. We cannot become different beings by clinging on to our personalities as they were formerly. Therefore it is essential for personality to be worked on in order to change into our more real selves (the selves we can become through the growth of essence, which acts as the vehicle for REAL I). This is another aspect of the present system of teaching which differentiates it so markedly from pseudo-esoteric systems. In such systems personality is built up still further, not diminished, and spiritual pride is added to the pride and vanity and self-conceit which already form such a large part of false personality.

The reader should therefore note all these points very

clearly. They separate true esotericism from the false as surely as dawn marks off night from day. There must always be a sacrifice for the sake of esotericism in our lives, and the sacrifice is in personality (or more correctly false personality) which must be starved out of existence in the process of inner transformation from the beings we are now into the beings we can become, and should be, if we live truly according to our essential nature.

Many earnest students of Eastern religious philosophy have heard about the conflict between the "lower self" and the "higher self" in the struggle for real inner development. They construe this struggle as one which goes on *in the personality*, whereby the better qualities in ourselves are pitted against the worse qualities, eventually—it is hoped—overcoming completely the bad qualities, whereby one will achieve one's aim in the quest for "spiritual salvation". Once we have come in touch with The Work, we realise that that viewpoint is entirely erroneous, and the reason why many earnest seekers for true inner understanding and spiritual development fail in their efforts. *There is no conflict which has to be fought out in the confines of the personality*. That is an erroneous conception. It is not *we* who have to fight the battle for spiritual progress, as it were. All we can do is to try to make personality increasingly more passive through work on ourselves, thereby enabling essence to become active and develop, and *then* REAL I can begin to make its presence felt in our lives. REAL I is the clue to the whole problem, and REAL I is already "there", at its own level, even if we are never aware of its existence. Once we are made aware of its existence, the effect it will have on us is to allow it to come into activity in our lives *by our work on personality*.

We must endeavour to understand what the personality really is, and how it *as a whole* is the one stumbling-block in the path of our inner expansion. We cannot *make* ourselves perfect. REAL I is already perfect—our link with the Divine.

It waits for the opportunity to come into our lives. By our
work on personality, the miracle will happen. It will occur
under its own laws. Those laws cannot be affected in any way
by struggle and activity of any kind. All we can do is co-
operate with the laws by trying to make personality
increasingly passive, as described in The Work teachings. The
whole situation is thus entirely different from that usually
understood by students of Eastern religious philosophy *who
have not the real key.*

This mistake, in varied forms, is also made by the vast
majority of the followers of the world's various orthodox
religious creeds. They also believe that they have to struggle
for "salvation". But, as clearly shown above, we hope, it is
not a struggle at all. It is just a question of letting REAL I
take over in our lives. It is wonderful to realise that REAL I
is already "there", perfect and complete, ready to take over
as soon as we provide for it the appropriate conditions.
Bring that thought to the surface many times a day. One will
be amply repaid. This links up with The Work teaching about
Self-Remembering which plays such an important part in The
Work as referred to in an earlier chapter. The Self we are
called upon to remember frequently during the day, in the
stress and conflict of everyday affairs, is REAL I, our *real
Self,* the Self which, ordinarily, we do not think of when under
the thrall of personality.

To conclude this chapter on personality and essence, we
must refer to two further important teachings of the Gurdjieff
system. These are those about Centres, and about Man
Number One, Two and Three. According to Gurdjieff we
have each a mental centre (in the mental body), an emotional
centre (in the emotional body), and an instinctive-moving
centre (in the physical body). Each of these centres is divided
into three parts : external, middle, and inner. The mental
centre deals with thought, the emotional with feeling, and
the instinctive-moving centre with the care and upkeep of the

body and all movement and activity, etc. There is also the sex centre, and we are told that very few people know how to use this centre properly.

The mental and emotional centres are divided into higher and lower spheres. In ordinary unevolved mankind (esoterically speaking) the higher mental and emotional centres are hardly ever contacted. These centres are fully operative on their level, but we never hear what they have to say or command, because living in the personality precludes our hearing them. One of the chief purposes of esoteric training is to enable us to contact our higher mental and emotional centres, and so allow them to guide and control our thinking and feeling. In people who are not esoterically developed, the mental and emotional bodies are in a rudimentary or nascent state. Through work on ourselves we can build up these bodies and so make contact with higher mental and emotional centres within us.

The teaching with regard to Man Nos. 1, 2, and 3 is that every human being is either chiefly physically-based, or emotionally-based, or mentally-based, that is to say, we all live chiefly through one centre. Some of us are therefore of the physical-instinctive type (Man No. 1), some the emotional type (Man No. 2) and some of the mental type (Man No. 3). We are all unbalanced and tend to live a one-sided kind of life, making it difficult for a person of one type to understand a person of another type.

The purpose of The Work is to make *balanced man* (or Man No. 4), i.e., a man who has *all* his centres developed and working in full harmony. In such a man the higher mental and emotional centres would also be fully operative, of course, thus co-ordinating all activity, whether physical, mental or emotional.

Another type of centre mentioned in The Work is the *magnetic centre*. In the teaching it is said that only persons with magnetic centre can appreciate what The Work is about and feel drawn to it. They feel the meaninglessness and emptiness of life as ordinarily lived, and are seeking for something different, they know not what. The average individual has not magnetic centre, and so The Work means nothing to him, even if explained carefully to him. He is dissatisfied with his life, of course, but feels that is simply because he is not getting all he can out of it in terms of money, position, power, or whatever else he may desire. Only those people with magnetic centre can appreciate that life as lived today is really worthless from the point of view of real satisfaction in living, and are ready to look elsewhere for the achievement of more worth-while aims, such as esotericism can provide.

The Work teachings about Man Nos. 1, 2, and 3, and the various centres, throw much light on the conduct of ordinary living, and therefore well repay earnest study. It is mainly the wrong functioning of the centres, as we are at present, which causes so much of the unbalance and disturbed living exhibited by the vast majority of people. To become Balanced Man, that is, Man No. 4, we have to adopt what is known in The Work terminology as The Fourth Way, which is really another name for The Work itself. The expression "The Fourth Way" is used because in the search for spiritual development up to now there have been three definite ways open to man for such development. These are : (1) The Way of the Fakir, who works essentially on the physical body; (2) The Way of the Monk, who works essentially on the emotional body; and (3) The Way of the Yogi, who works essentially on the mental body. Under the System we are discussing, man is encouraged to work on all his various bodies simultaneously, in order to achieve the position of Balanced Man, No. 4 Man. Thus the use of the term : *The Fourth Way.*

CHAPTER VIII

Man as a Self-Developing Organism

We have said that the basic requisite for esoteric development is that man must change himself, but this pre-supposes that he is capable of change. This is a most important and profound statement, as we shall see, if we study it carefully. What would be the good of saying that man must change himself if he is incapable of change? In the Gurdjieff system it is laid down as a cardinal principle that man is *a self-developing organism,* i.e. something capable of internal growth or change. In other words, as man is he is incomplete, or imperfect; but he has something within him which makes it possible for him to become complete or perfect. The sole purpose of The Work is to enable man to achieve this objective through the measures we have discussed, and others we shall be referring to in later chapters.

It is said in The Work teaching that man, as he now is, feeds life, i.e., that he is simply the tool of life and Nature. The fact that he is a self-developing organism indicates that within him lies a power—dormant at present—which can come into activity and transform his whole life and being, by making it possible for REAL I to come into activity and take command. If we accept the truth of this statement, we have to accept the further fact that some power much greater than man has sown the seeds for such inner development within him. This leads us on to the consideration of something of the greatest importance—*a belief in the existence of PURPOSE in the Universe.*

Nineteenth-century science took the view that the Universe was meaningless and purposeless—"a fortuitous concourse of atoms", and most scientific thought up to the present day reflects this same viewpoint. There are, however, scientists who have subscribed to the view that there *is* meaning and purpose in the workings of the Universe. These are the more intuitive type of scientist or physicist, such as Einstein, Eddington, Whitehead, and the like. These men have not been carried away by the seeming triumphs and achievements of the scientific method, and man's "conquest of Nature", so-called. They have remained humble in the face of what they realise to be truly sublime and awe-inspiring in the handiwork of creation, as depicted in the myriad material forms included in this remarkable Universe. Such men do not regard matter as something merely material and inert. They realise that it is the vehicle for something far greater, i.e., intelligence or spirit, which decrees the scientific laws under which all material bodies operate, from electron and atom upwards. They regard matter as having a consciousness of its own in the way in which it combines with other material forms or is repelled by them.

This is the viewpoint of Esotericists right down through the ages. Esotericism posits that CONSCIOUSNESS is at the basis of everything created, its source being rooted in the Divine Reality which has brought the Universe into existence, its manifestations being everywhere. This means that the Universe is the product of *intelligence,* which is called in The Work "Greater Mind", the Seen always being the product of the Unseen. It is the purpose of all created things to try to develop their consciousness to the greatest possible extent within the particular order or species or genus. The degree of conscious development possible for the mineral kingdom is very strictly limited, indeed, and that for the plant kingdom not very much more; while for the animal kingdom, outside man, it is only a little more still, in type and degree.

That means to say that in these realms of Nature conscious development is limited to being as fully alive as possible in things at the original level of Creation. For example, a thing, mineral, vegetable or animal, can only be a diamond, or a rose, or a cabbage, or a mouse, or a tiger, for instance, if it is created that way. The sole avenue for development in these things lies in each striving to be as perfect a diamond or a rose or cabbage, or mouse or tiger as conditions will permit. *In the case of a man, however, things are different !* In his case there is the possibility of the development of consciousness to a degree which transforms him entirely, marking him off completely from esoterically undeveloped mankind.

The Work teaching about man being a self-developing organism has the most profound meaning and significance for those who have "the ears to hear and the eyes to see". It shows us that we are part of a great Cosmic Plan which has the development of ever-greater CONSCIOUSNESS as its prime purpose. When one takes up the task of trying to work on oneself, in line with the teachings of Esotericism, then one becomes a conscious collaborator with this great Cosmic Plan. One is then working in harmony with the Universe, instead of in opposition to it, as is now the case with the vast majority of human beings. The mineral kingdom, the plant kingdom, and the animal kingdom all work in harmony with the Universal Plan, but unconsciously. Man *only* (of all creation on this earth) is capable of working consciously in co-operation with the Universal Plan. This is a most wonderful destiny ! Yet, without the key provided by Esotericism, mankind in general is completely unaware of that destiny. Hence its inability to secure real happiness for itself in ordinary living. It is looking in the wrong direction for its fulfilment.

When we realise we are part of universal life, and capable of becoming conscious co-operators with that universal life, a purpose and meaning is given to existence which ordinary living in the personality cannot provide. Real happiness and contentment in living are only possible to those treading the path of The Work, and they are achieved in increasing measure the more nearly one comes to the full realisation of the task in hand. It is the reward of rewards, and all this is what Christ referred to when he spoke about "The Kingdom of Heaven" in the Gospels. It is not a kingdom of the future (of a future life to be lived in an after-death world). It has reference to life lived *here and now* on this earth, but in conscious co-operation with our Creative Source.

We have just said that the development of consciousness is the keynote of all creation. In The Work teaching there is frequent reference to what is called "The Conscious Circle of Humanity". This is a term which signifies those beings who through work on themselves have attained the status whereby REAL I is fully operative within them. That such beings do exist is part of the teaching of all esoteric systems, and in the East they are known as " The Masters of Wisdom". It is they who have charge of the real inner development of mankind, under the hierarchical system through which the Cosmos is governed. They seek to influence man in every way they can, using special Groups and Churches as a focus for their efforts, through the channels of religion (in its true sense), art, literature, philosophy, etc. They also send out teachers in various guises to help erring mankind, and all esoteric systems owe their inception to this "Conscious Circle of Humanity". It is part of The Work teaching that the influence of such directors of conscious evolution cannot reach us direct at our level; the influences have to be "stepped-down" in order to be understood by us; and that has given rise to The Work teaching about A., B., and C. influences.

A. influences are those coming direct from life, i.e., from the factors and circumstances which control everyday living and impinge directly on the personality. Such A. influences are environment, education, social factors of all kinds, etc., and it is through their constant impingement on us that our day-to-day living is affected. We react to A. influences all the time.

C. influences are those which "The Conscious Circle of Humanity" pour down on us through their agents and agencies, of whatever kind. These have to be stepped-down into B. influences before we on this earth-plane can understand them (in so far as they are understandable by us) except when transmitted through Esoteric Schools which can receive C. influences without distortion. The Gospels are an example of C. influences which have been stepped-down into B. influences; and so are the words of The Buddha, of Mahomet, and of all real religious teachers, sages and seers. All great works of art, all great literature, drama, etc., are also examples of B. influences; and so are all esoteric schools and systems and their literature. If we have magnetic centre we can be drawn to B. influences and so begin to be drawn away from the sway of A. influences, and this again can be said to be the sole purpose of Esotericism (put into other words).

When we realise that we are part of a great Cosmic Plan or Design, and learn at last what our own rôle in the drama is to be, i.e., that of self-development of inner powers and potentialities leading to greater and greater CONSCIOUS-NESS, then we know that—at long last—we have found our real niche in life. Before that we were aliens in a foreign world, although we were not conscious of the fact. We were conscious that life seemed a mere chaos, something entirely meaningless and devoid of purpose. That feeling we had had for a long time (all those with magnetic centre, that is). So that when, at last, through one means or another we are brought into touch with Esotericism, and begin to understand its teachings, we feel that at last we have "come home". We have at long last entered a world which does begin to make sense. The farther we tread along that path, the more certain do we become that everything belonging to it makes more and more sense, despite what the denizens of the ordinary everyday world may think or say.

We *know* we have found the key, because we can tell by our inner feeling. We know that at long last we have found the way to our real self, which by living immersed in the personality, we have been prevented from knowing. We can appreciate the supreme value of teachings that man is a self-developing organism, and those about the "Conscious Circle of Humanity", and of A., B., and C. influences, etc. They make life meaningful and purposeful. In very truth we can say that in such teachings we are given keys to real living which nothing in the ordinary everyday world can provide, no matter how much we may be prepared to spend for their attainment. These teachings are beyond price and have no price.

CHAPTER IX

NEGATIVE EMOTIONS

WE wish to say now something about what in The Work are called *negative emotions*. This is a teaching of fundamental importance, and marks off very signally the difference between what we have termed Esoteric Psychology, and ordinary Psychology. So far we have not said much about Krishnamurti's particular teachings; these are being reserved for special mention later. What we are saying now, however, has direct reference to his views, as the reader will realize later.

According to The Work teaching about emotional centre, we are told that the Higher Emotional Centre is fully operative and active on its *own* level, but we at our level are unable to contact it or hear or feel what it has to tell us. The Lower Emotional Centre is where we function daily in our emotional life. It is—according to The Work teaching—composed mainly of negative emotions of various kinds. Negative emotions are such feelings as fear, anger, jealousy, hatred, impatience, worry, self-pity, etc. It is said that they fill our emotional life and that we are their constant prey.

If we examine ourselves, through the technique of self-observation, and are really candid and do not try to self-justify, we can see that The Work teaching is perfectly true. Our lives *are* full of the negative emotions, which crowd in on us throughout the day, as this or that temporary "I" takes command of us. It is through work on ourselves that we should try to note the existence of the negative emotions within us, *and to try not to identify with them.* The more we can become conscious of them, and separate from them, the less influence over us can they have, so that gradually we can become entirely free of them.* While the process of inner cleansing of the lower emotional centre is taking place, preparation and accommodation is being made for the influences of the higher emotional centre to be heard by us. It will be readily understood, therefore, that by progressively cleansing the emotional centre of all negative emotions we can make the quickest progress towards esoteric development.

When we consider to what extent such emotions as fear, worry, anger, jealousy, hatred, impatience, self-pity, etc., plague our lives, we can readily realize how amazing it would be if we could become entirely free from them. It may seem a herculean task, and so in a way it is; but we always have to bear in mind that in The Work we do not do anything ourselves. *We cannot do,* remember! Once we embark upon The Work all we can do is to try to make personality more and more passive. *The Work does the rest.*

One of the best ways of rendering the personality more passive is by observing our negative emotions and trying not to identify with them. The more we can recognize negative emotions at work, and try to separate from them (by declaring to ourselves that they are not *us,* but only aspects of our false personality), then the more scope, the more room in emotional centre, will there be for the higher emotional centre to become active. Emotional centre purified allows higher emotional centre to operate in and through us. That means the emergence of such positive emotions as awe, wonder, appreciation of beauty (and of the mystery

---

* Genuine sorrow and suffering are *not* negative emotions. They are of positive value, because they are related to the *real* part of ourselves, not our false personality. Feelings such as kindliness, gratitude, devotion, sympathy, etc. are also more positive types of emotion, although not strictly positive in The Work sense, because really positive emotions are very rare. Pity is generally not a positive emotion, but most often negative.

of creation), compassion, real love (not the psuedo love of the personality), etc. These real and *more genuine* emotions will gradually take over the place of the former all-embracing negative ones.

It is therefore easy to see how much richer and more worth-while our emotional lives will become in every way. The more positive emotions come from the inner part of the emotional centre, the negative emotions from the outer part. Our feelings about life and about ourselves will be transformed, as part of the inner transformation which The Work is effecting. Reverence for Nature brings with it the feeling that we are not strangers in the Universe, as we may feel when shut up within the confines of the personality. We begin to feel at home with the stars and their constellations, and are drawn to study about them and ponder over the mystery which enshrouds them. Our feelings begin to reach out in all directions, into the smallest as into the greatest, and everything we see or hear or read about has a *positive* interest for us, within its own field or realm. In other words, as negative emotions are worked on and separated from, and more positive emotions start to fill their places, we actually feel that we are beginning *to live* at last. While we are the prey of negative emotions *we merely exist*. Only when positive emotions from higher emotional centre begin to fill the places formerly held by negative emotions do we begin to feel something new and different stirring within us : something which makes life really worth-while, because we are living it with the right part of ourselves and not the wrong part, as hitherto.

According to The Work teachings we are not born with negative emotions; they are sown in us through imitation of our elders during infancy, and by the gradual encroachment of the everyday world, with its false values and objectives. By the time adulthood is reached the emotional centre is a mass of negative emotions, as already indicated, and in the vast majority of cases we live out the rest of our lives entirely

within their thrall. We are literally the prisoners of our
negative emotions, as we can easily discover through some
careful and non-critical self-observation.

Of all negative emotions it is The Work teaching that *fear*
is the most deep-seated. The personality craves for security
in a very insecure world; it—the product of perishable matter
and doomed to eventual dissolution—demands continuity for
itself and permanence, which it is quite unable to secure for
itself. Therefore, the personality's basic reaction to life is *fear*.
All of its frantic efforts are directed towards the assuagement
of its basic fear, of which it is quite unaware, superficially.
Closely allied to the fundamental fear-complex within the
personality is violence. Whenever the personality feels itself
threatened in any way, or has its wishes or desires thwarted,
its basic reaction to such factors is violence. Indeed, we can
say that the chief purpose of esoteric training is to exorcise
violence from our lives. If we can attain this objective, we
can be assured that we have very nearly reached the stage
when REAL I will be in permanent possession of us.

In his teachings Krishnamurti has a great deal to say about
the overcoming of violence. He sees it as at the bottom of
practically everything connected with the activities of the
personality. That in itself shows how close are his views,
basically, to those of the Gurdjieff system, although they may
seem very much the reverse. But that is *only superficially*. By
his views about and attitude towards violence Krishnamurti
shows very clearly indeed that his objective is exactly the
same as that of The Work.

The earnest and sincere people who believe that we can
abolish war and establish an era of lasting world peace merely
by signing conventions or agreements, have not realised that
the key to the solution of the problem lies in the overcoming
of violence *within ourselves*. It is a curious fact that many
pacifists appear to be very violent people, indeed, especially
when their pet views are objected to or argued against. They

have not the slightest idea of how violent they are in themselves, yet they expect other people to give up their violence in the interests of world peace. We all agree that world peace is a great and worthy objective; but what most people do not seem to appreciate at all is that until *all of us* are prepared to give up our violence, there cannot possibly be lasting peace in the world.

We are not likely to give up our violence until we can begin to see what effect it is having on our inner state—as a result of non-critical self-observation—in conjunction with all the other negative emotions. Thus the relinquishing of violence can only be achieved as part of *work on ourselves* under the aegis of Esotericism. We cannot give up violence in a moment. We can only do so when we really realize the need for working against it—in all its varied and multifarious manifestations—in our own lives. War is merely the manifestation of violence on a mass-scale.

We have already referred in this chapter to insecurity. Let us add that the personality craves security, because it feels itself basically insecure, and that gives rise to the emotion of fear, as already indicated. What we have to realize, however, is that there can never be real security for anyone on this earth. Insecurity is an inevitable fundamental factor in our lives. When one begins to work on oneself one is ready to accept insecurity and not be affected by it. Once we are prepared to accept insecurity as basic to our lives we cease to worry about it. Much of the fear which previously took up so much of the emotional centre (in various forms) no longer affects us. Imagine what a tremendous gain is this one fact, in itself. The more we accept consciously the presence of insecurity, the less important does it become. It is a curious fact that the more people worry about insecurity the more it dogs them, whereas the less they care about it the less they are worried by it. This, in a way, is only the working of one of the cosmic laws about which mankind in general is so ignorant. It says that the more we worry about a thing the more we attract it; the less we worry about it the less we attract it.

The reader can easily observe how that sort of reasoning can be applied to nearly all the negative emotions which together continuously plague our lives. It is only a way of working on oneself to free the emotional centre of the vast mass of negative emotions with which it is cluttered, so paving the way for influences from the higher emotional centre to filter down and make their presence felt. Some people have never felt a positive emotion in their lives; if they ever did so they would be amazed at the difference in feeling which it engenders. Conscious work on negative emotions makes the entrance of positive emotions more and more certain, as each day passes. We leave it to the reader to appreciate what this will mean in due course, as work on oneself progresses. It means an entire revolution in feeling. We begin to become *attuned* to the Universe, because the existence of negative emotions in the emotional centre previously made all possibility of such attunement impossible.

CHAPTER X

INTERNAL AND EXTERNAL ACCOUNTS

THE greatest of all factors in regard to the personality is love of itself. Self-love, as it is called in The Work, is another basic factor in human life, so long as our centre of gravity lies within the personality. It cannot be otherwise, because the personality can only think of itself. Selfishness is its chief characteristic, as we must all recognize. Even when we maintain we are being unselfish, on occasion, truthful analysis of our actions or feelings will make us realize that our unselfishness was only selfishness disguised. This is true even about love. Ordinary love of the personality can never be anything but selfish. Real love is a positive emotion and is truly unselfish. It can come only from a higher inner level than that of the self or personality. We may have felt such an emotion occasionally, but only on very special and rare occasions, and when called forth by something greater than the everyday happenings of existence.

Linked up inevitably with self-love and our besetting sin of selfishness is what is termed by The Work *making accounts*. We go about thinking that this or that person owes us something (in the sense of not having treated us properly in accordance with what we feel is our due). Or we may feel that we are being belittled by this or that group of people or by a certain organization, and so on. Our lives are full of this kind of account-making. We feel we are being slighted, or overlooked, or not given our due, etc. Self-observation will

71

soon reveal the truth of all this making of accounts. This is another important phase of work for those wishing to tread the esoteric path: *we have to stop making inner accounts.*

All account-making springs from False Personality; through hurt vanity or pride, or wounded self-conceit, etc. If we wish to stop the all-too-human trait of account-making, we must begin to work on false personality in a big way. No longer must we take it for granted that the world and other people owe us anything, i.e., deference, gratitude for favours done, or whatever it may be. We must start wiping the slate clean of all such inner accounting. We must realize that if people do not take us at our own valuation, that that valuation is only false in any case, for it springs from our false personality. If people do not think we are as wonderful, or as righteous, or loveable, or important, or whatever, as we think we are, then leave them to their opinion. That is the only way to work on ourselves in this connection. By doing so we begin to lessen the habit of inner account-making, with a most gratifying result in feeling inwardly very much better and cleaner.

Instead of being cluttered up continually with thoughts and feelings of how badly we are being treated, or how malignly our true value is being overlooked, and so on and so forth, we can start to accept the fact that we are not as important in other people's eyes as we had previously imagined. This can be a very salutary experience. It quietens us inside, and makes us more ready to appreciate that what other people may think or feel about us has little real reference to what we really are in ourselves. *What we are* no one can take away from us. The only thing other people can take away from us is our sense of false pride in ourselves, and our false conceit about ourselves, which spring from false personality.

Closely connected with our sin of account-making is what is known in The Work as "Inner Talking", which is dealt with more fully in a later chapter. Let us say this, now : we are very frequently talking to ourselves about other people and the disgraceful way they treat us, or slight us, or avoid us, or whatever it may be. This inward talking is another aspect of the making of inner accounts. The amount of vital energy such inner talking can consume is amazing. We can be literally drained of energy through this practice; and a great many people spend most of their days doing such inner talking. It is constant and ceaseless in the vast majority of us, as uncritical self-observation will soon reveal. By working against the making of inner accounts through following The Work teachings, and putting a stop to inner talking, we shall find that we have abundant energy available for more constructive and worth-while effort. Thus we gain enormously by this type of work on ourselves.

The converse of the making of inner accounts against other people, with its concomitant of inner talking, is what is known in The Work as "External Considering". In making inner accounts we consider only ourselves (e.g., what other people owe to us). The reverse process, therefore, is to consider *what we owe to other people*. Ordinarily we are so filled with thoughts about what other people owe to us, that we never stop to think what we may owe to them. The Work teaches that the very best way in which to work against inner account-making is to adopt the reverse process, of thinking about what we owe to others.

When we are able to view the matter in that light, there will be a great reversal within us. Instead of there being, as it were, some inner point which is forever seeking to draw into itself (from the outside world) everything it possibly can (e.g., that feeling of *me, me, me, all the time*) the reverse process comes into action. We begin to *give out* to other people, in thought, consideration, thanks, sympathy, kindliness, and so forth. Strange as it may seem, the more we do give out in this way, the richer do we begin to feel inside. It is rather a strange paradox, because formerly, when we tried to draw everything into ourselves, we felt meaner and meaner inside (i.e., less and less rich in ourselves), now, when we begin the reverse process of giving out, we begin to feel a new richness coming into our lives, a richness which grows increasingly as we cultivate the idea of External Considering.

There are many ways, indeed, in which external considering can be practised. In *Psychological Commentaries* Dr. Nicoll gives innumerable illustrations of external considering. It is an essential part of the process of *work on ourselves*. But external considering must never be tinged with patronage, such as represented by the "look how good I am in doing this for you" sort of expression. That is not external considering. Real external considering springs from a feeling of humility within ourselves, a genuine feeling of what we owe to others as fellow human-beings. It has nothing to do with condescension, or sham piety, or righteousness, or the pharisaical doing of "good works", or anything of a like nature. All such feelings and acts which spring from them are part of the activity of false personality. This brings us to The Work teaching about *inner taste*.

According to this teaching, when we begin to work on ourselves genuinely, we soon develop a feeling within us which tells us directly and immediately whether anything we are doing is genuine or otherwise. This feeling has nothing to do with conventional views about conduct, or conventional morality, or ethics. It is a feeling which derives from *true conscience within us*, and should not be confused with *acquired conscience*, which has its origin in environment, upbringing, education, etc. Acquired conscience is grafted on to us gradually, from birth, and so overlays real conscience, which lies buried beneath it. It is only by work on ourselves, and the dethronement of false personality (with which acquired conscience is allied) that real conscience can begin to make its presence felt. This is known in The Work as *Inner Taste*. We have a feeling about a thing, and that feeling tells us right away whether what we are doing or thinking is right or wrong. It is right or wrong for *us*, and not for the next person, of course. Hence it has nothing to do with conventional morality, which makes things right or wrong for all of us, irrespective of what we may be or may be striving to be. The Work teaching says that real conscience is really the same in all of us, so that what it says, through Inner Taste, is applicable in general to all mankind. It can vary widely, of course, in the direction it may take in any individual case, being relative to circumstances, environmental factors, personal needs and responsibilities, etc.

At this point it may be well to refer to The Work teaching called *Chief Feature*. We have said, early in this chapter, that our besetting sin is self-love, and that the personality is the epitome of selfishness. According to The Work teaching the very core of this self-love and selfishness within the personality is what is known as Chief Feature. Chief Feature can be taken to be that central point within us around which all the other qualities or traits of the personality revolve. Chief Feature ramifies through all of them, yet remains invisible itself. Thus we may go through our whole life with no awareness of our chief feature, although other people may be well aware of it. They see it at work within us, but we ourselves are incapable of doing so, because of the imaginations and phantasies about ourselves in which we are habitually immersed.

Only after long and painful work on oneself can that chief feature be at last revealed. We are told that this revelation comes as a profound shock to us because we never realized before that we are like what we really are. This revelation of chief feature takes place, therefore, only when the candidate is at a sufficient stage of inner development of being capable of standing the shock. If it were revealed too early the effect might be catastrophic. Once chief feature has been revealed and brought right out into the light of day, the false personality is ready to fall to pieces, because it is chief feature which keeps it in being.

Our chief feature can vary considerably, according to temperament, character, etc., but it is always related either to lust for power, accumulation of wealth (in its many and varied forms), sex in its many and varied guises, desire for dominance over others (either materially or through the mind and emotions), and similar characteristics of human personality which are powerful enough to dominate the thought and energy of individual men and women without their conscious awareness. Technically, there are said to be eight different categories of Chief Feature, but basically they are fear, sex, lying, pride and greed.

CHAPTER XI

INNER TALKING: ATTITUDES: AND PICTURES

WE wish now to say something about three subjects of considerable importance to the student embarking on the esoteric path, for which The Work has special names. These are : Inner Talking, Attitudes, and Pictures, to which we shall refer in turn.

Inner talking is the continuous conversation we always have with ourselves whenever we are alone. Immediately we are by ourselves, the inner conversation begins : 99 per cent of it is concerned with our supposed grievances, personal upsets, problems, intentions, and so forth. For example, we continually go over in our mind what so-and-so said to us, and why he did not treat us as he should have done, and what we ought to have said to him but did not. Or, why people think they can do what they like with us at work because we are the sort that tries not to shirk our job and so consequently advantage is taken of us. Or, why our wife or children never seem to respect us sufficiently. Or, what so-and-so said to somebody else about A. or B. or C. or someone else we know. And so on *ad infinitum*. We all know what inner talking is, because it is something we all indulge in when by ourselves, and it is our constant companion during our waking hours. By it and in it we subject the various occurrences of the day (or of the past) to a continual going over, trying to show ourselves to ourselves in the best possible light; making excuses for remarks or situations in regard to which we felt at the time we had not particularly distinguished ourselves. In short, through and by inner talking we conduct a campaign of self-justification and self-adoration whereby we keep ourselves at the highest degree of our personal estimation.

Inner talking is, indeed, the handmaid of self-love and the cult of the personality. According to The Work teaching about this particular subject it is one of the most potent ways of losing force. The more we persist in this continual inner conversation with ourselves (which is a monologue rather than a dialogue) the more force do we lose, because inner talking is one of the most negative of all the ways in which the personality acts in its day-to-day conduct of life. We drain away force as we indulge in inner talk. Once we are made aware of the fact, and study our inner talking, we become aware of how true this is. The people who do most inner talking are those who continually complain how tired or lacking in vitality they are, and such people are always prone to develop whatever disease may be rampant at any time, apart from being saddled already with one or more chronic maladies.

One of the first steps towards Self-Knowledge is to become aware of the existence of inner talking, and what it does to us. *We must resolve to stop it.* This is a very difficult task and it can only be successfully tackled very gradually; but it is something every student of The Work has to work on continually.

The subject of inner talking is bound up most intimately, we find, with what The Work calls *requirements*. We are full of requirements, but until we become consciously aware of the fact, we are blissfully unaware of the existence within us of this psychological disturber of the peace. The Work refers to, as requirements, those conditions we mentally impose upon others (and upon the world in general) whereby we take it for granted that certain things are owed to us. That is to say, we feel that life should provide us with certain amenities to living, with certain favours, privileges, etc., although we do not regard the matter in just that light. Indeed, we do not see it in that way at all. For the requirements are really quite outside our conscious thought. We just take them for granted. When they are not forthcoming, we begin to feel annoyed or upset, and thus begins that constant stream of inner talking about which we have been speaking.

For example, we may feel that certain things are owed to us, such as respect from others; that other people should like us; that we should be happy always; that we should have pleasant work, congenial home life, etc.; that external things should not disturb our comfort or enjoyment; and so on. As already said, we do not explicitly state these demands to ourselves. Indeed, we are not consciously aware that we make such demands on life. We certainly do, however, and when our requirements are not met, we begin to inner talk, because we feel that life and the world are not treating us rightly. Therefore, we feel we have a definite inner grievance, and we become full of self-pity. It is precisely the inner grievances, in whatever form they may come to us, which are the basis of inner talking. We continually talk to ourselves about them, losing force all the time, and feel that we are very badly treated.

The Work teachings give definite instructions about inner talking and how it can be combated or short-circuited. One of the most important ways by which this can be achieved is by *reducing our requirements*. The less we expect from life and from other people, the less cause will there be for us to be annoyed or upset if what we require is not forthcoming. Indeed, it can be said categorically that from the esoteric standpoint the individual who can cut his requirements to nil is well on the way to the achievement of his esoteric goal. If we expect nothing from life, we cannot be disappointed. That puts an end to all feeling of grievance, and so inner talking is cut off at its source. It takes a really "big" person to demand no requirements from life, and this, in itself, is a sure indication of where an individual is, in the esoteric scale.

For a fuller development of the subject of Inner Talking the reader is referred to Dr. Nicoll's *Commentaries,* in which the theme is treated from many angles.

We now wish to say something about what in The Work is referred to as *attitudes.* Attitudes may be briefly defined as our habitual modes of thought, our habitual way of thinking and believing. For instance, we have our own special attitudes, peculiar to ourselves, upon all sorts of topics, ranging from religion to politics, sex, work, leisure and anything else. We each have our own manifold attitudes upon these and all other subjects, in which we are encased as in a sort of armour. We regard those attitudes as different aspects of *ourselves,* not realising in the slightest that they are merely mental garments which we don and take off, according to circumstances, and that they have no real relationship to us, fundamentally. They are simply guises of the personality, and mainly of the false personality at that, built up over the years, through education, custom, tradition, etc.

The more sincerely we take these attitudes as honest expressions of ourselves, the more are we led astray in our understanding of what we really are. In short, attitudes are among the chief stumbling-blocks to Self-Knowledge. Therefore, if we wish to attain Self-Knowledge, we have to become aware of our various attitudes, through careful and consistent self-observation and study, and so gradually be able to divest ourselves of them. The way will be paved *then* for our more essential nature to show itself and express itself. *Then* what we say or do will be influenced directly by this more real part of ourselves, and not be just an attitude—a gramophone record put on and played mechanically by the false personality. When we become more conscious of ourselves, more "self-aware", it will be easy to see these attitudes taking command of us, according to the circumstances of the moment. In the ordinary way we are not aware of them, we simply regard them as different aspects of ourselves and so identify with them completely.

Closely related to this teaching of The Work about attitudes is the teaching about *pictures*. Pictures may be regarded as our habitual ways of viewing ourselves. When we think about ourselves we have pictures of ourselves as being this or that sort of person; a person always being kind and considerate to others, for instance, or always being "tough", or always being good company, or always being hard working, and so forth. There are a large variety of such pictures which we hold about ourselves, closely related, as just said, to attitudes. We go through life believing thoroughly in such pictures, even though to other people they are quite untrue. The point is that *we* believe they are true, that they represent us as we really are, and we bask in such pictures and get lost in them, and so gain a completely false evaluation of ourselves. We think we are "such and such" a person, when to others we are entirely different.

For example, we may have a picture of ourself as being a very reasonable person, always open to argument and persuasion, according to what is right; whereas other people may see us as a very unreasonable, and very dictatorial and bullying type. Or we may have a picture of ourselves as being very open-handed and generous, whereas other people may think we are quite mean and parsimonious. This sort of thing is of quite common occurrence, and only shows us how little we really know of ourselves, even as to what we are like where other people are concerned. We have an entirely wrong idea of ourselves through the pictures in our minds. Therefore, quite apart from the fact that we identify with our personalities and have no idea of what lies beyond and behind that *façade,* we have no idea of what our personalities are *really* like in themselves. The whole situation is clouded by the pictures and attitudes which comprise so much of our mental furniture.

We have lost touch with the reality about ourselves, in other words, even though that reality is about the self which is only the superficial covering of ourselves. Perhaps this may seem a little involved, but in any case it only shows what we have to learn about ourselves before any real Self-Knowledge is possible. It is an extremely arduous and difficult process, as befits something which is of such vital importance to us. If the attainment of Self-Knowledge were easy, there would be nothing to be gained. Being what it is, it *must* be difficult. What we have been saying in the present chapter gives some idea of the difficulties we have to contend with in unravelling the skein of our psychological make-up. Incidentally, it also shows us how vastly different is esoteric from ordinary psychology. The two are really poles apart.

CHAPTER XII

LEVELS OF BEING

IT is now time to examine another fundamentally important teaching of The Work, and that is with regard to *levels of being*. In the everyday world there are various grades and distinctions of people, according to birth, rank, power, wealth, and so on. Such diversities or divisions of people have no real fundamental value. The only real thing which differentiates people from one another is their level of being.

The Work teaches that we are all at different levels of being, according to our *inner development*, so that *external* differences due to wealth, position, education, etc., have no bearing whatsoever on the level of being of one person relative to another. This is a truth many people will recognize intuitively. We have all had the experience of meeting people who seem quite humble and even inconspicuous in themselves, yet about whom we feel something which distinguishes them immediately from other people. These men or women have "something different", and that something different springs from what they are *in themselves*. It has nothing to do with external or outside factors of any kind. Such people have a degree of inner development which is immediately felt by those with whom they come into contact who have the ability to sense it. The more we work on ourselves, through esoteric teaching, the more does our level of being develop. It is an inevitable process, and the only way in which we can grow internally.

According to The Work teaching, level of being should be

related to level of knowledge, because the resultant of the two
is our level of understanding. Understanding is the most
prized quality we can ever possess. Understanding is synonymous with wisdom. To be really wise is the characteristic of
people who have worked on themselves through esoteric training, and attained a very high level of being accordingly, with
which is also related a very high level of knowledge. To
arrive at one's level of understanding (or wisdom) we have to
add together the level of knowledge and the level of being,
and then divide by two. It will be readily seen, therefore, that
a man or woman may have a very high level of knowledge,
but not a very high level of being, with the consequence that
they have not a very high level of understanding or wisdom.
Their knowledge may be great, but their understanding is not.
We can see this with eminent men of science. Their level of
knowledge may be relatively enormous; but, because they are
materialists and deny any meaning or purpose in the Universe,
their level of being is very low. Therefore, their level of
understanding or wisdom is quite poor despite their vast
knowledge. It is the same with people in many other spheres
of activity. Their level of knowledge is quite out of propor-
tion to their level of being, so that as a consequence their level
of understanding is insignificant, despite their pre-eminence
in their particular field or avocation.

The reverse is the case with the people who have quite a
high level of being but not a very high level of knowledge,
such as simple people who live close to Nature, and have a
deep intuitive awareness of the wonder and miracle of
creation, like many old-fashioned gardeners. These persons
have something within them which is very fine, as one can
readily sense when talking to them; but their level of knowledge (apart from their own work) is very poor, with the result
that their level of understanding is quite low, despite their
relatively high level of being, and their particular knowledge
of their craft.

The reader should readily observe how important is this teaching of The Work. It shows us how to appraise people at their true valuation, and not in accordance with the world's values. It also shows how important it is when trying to work on ourselves to work on knowledge as well as being. When turning to Esotericism too many people think that development of being is all-important. It is very important, of course, but development of knowledge is very important, too, for the reasons just explained. Without the requisite development of knowledge to keep pace with our development of being we can never reach a high level of understanding or wisdom; and, as already said, it is only understanding that counts in real esoteric development. Not just level of being alone.

Linked up with the question of understanding is the type of mentality we possess. Without some measure of real understanding we tend to view the world and its problems from a very matter-of-fact level, missing entirely anything which is not readily revealed to the everyday mind and senses. We tend towards what in The Work is called the Yes or No type of mind. This is the type of mentality which thinks it is possible to give definite answers to every problem, and demands a categorical "yes" or "no" to every question. As we progress in The Work, however, and our level of both knowledge and being grow, with the consequent development of real understanding, we find it increasingly difficult to give definite answers to questions, or to demand definite answers from others. We begin to realize that things are far more complicated and involved than we had thought previously, with the result that we no longer seek for, or expect, prompt answers to every problem.

We may say, therefore, that the best way to assess the level of understanding of any individual is to observe how he reacts to questions. If he is the type who expects a definite "yes" or "no", his level of understanding is very poor. The higher the level of understanding, the less likely will be the individual to expect that sort of thing. The same applies to having opinions about subjects. The more that people have definite and "mass-produced" and ready-made opinions about things, the less deep is their level of understanding; because the more we really know and understand, the more do we realise that ready-made opinions are worthless. There are so many factors involved in what may seem the simplest of problems, that ready-made answers are often quite useless. It is not inferred that we should be unable to act promptly where the need arises; but that the more our understanding has developed, through work on both knowledge and being, the more fully shall we appreciate what may be involved in whatever we are doing or intend to do. The result will be that we shall be far more ready for any untoward consequences of our actions than those people who think the problem to be quite simple. In other words, real understanding cuts out much of the unpleasant reactions which often attend our efforts in response to the challenge of life; and that surely is the hallmark of real wisdom.

Closely linked with the question of levels of being is The Work teaching about *scale*. Owing to the fact that science is largely materialistic in character and outlook, the tendency has developed of regarding all phenomena as being possibly different in magnitude but being more or less all on the same scale. No allowance is made for the possibility that some types of phenomena may be on a different level from others, and consequently requiring different ways of handling.

This can perhaps be observed most easily in the attitude of the majority of scientists to the phenomena of the branch of study which comes under the heading of Psychical Research. Here we have a body of knowledge which is rapidly gaining more and more publicity and attention, and which obviously requires an entirely different approach from that needed for dealing with purely physical phenomena. Most scientists, however, refuse to pay any heed or give any credence to

Psychical Research simply because it does not conform to the same type of measurements and calculations to which scientists can subject material phenomena. Such scientists refuse to admit that here they are dealing with another level or scale of being in the material world. This sort of attitude explains why "Science" as a whole has for so long not seen eye to eye with "Religion".

It is not to be inferred that all scientists are antagonistic to religion. The great challenge of Science to Religion in the nineteenth century was purely over the question of scale. Scientists wanted to apply exactly the same rules and regulations to the phenomena of religion as they did to those of material phenomena. When they found that this was impossible, they turned their backs on religion and declared its teachings to be unsound. That is a very good example of refusal to admit that there is scale in the Universe and in man's relation to it. Not that we would defend all of what passes or has passed for religion; far from it. But to assume that religion can be tested by the same methods of assessment as the manifestations of the material world is surely ridiculous.

Once we admit the existence of scale or levels of being in the Universe as well as in man, we are in an entirely different world from that inhabited by most people. Everything takes on far more meaning and significance, and there is room for far more wonder and mystery in everything. The people who think that everything can be reduced to mathematical symbols, for instance, live in a closed world wherein mystery, wonder and miracle have no place. The more we admit the existence of scale and levels of being both in ourselves and in the surrounding Universe, the more deeply do we feel things, and accordingly the more value and significance do we obtain from life. We begin to really *live*, whereas these other people just stagnate. They are quite dead *within*, however much they may seem alive on the surface. In other words, to live more abundantly we must be ready to accept the existence of scale and levels of being; otherwise we are the "living dead" about whom Christ had so much to say. Such people live in a dead world, because a world without scale and levels of being is indeed dead. Life cannot possibly function without scale and levels of being; they are part of its *modus operandi*.

There is a very old esoteric saying to the effect that man is the *microcosm* and God the *Macrocosm*. This means that reflected in man are the same factors and qualities with which the vast Universe is endowed. "As above, so below" is another esoteric saying which carries with it the same viewpoint. These sayings have direct reference to the existence of scale and levels of being both in man and in the Cosmos. If it were not so, man would be lacking in any ability to contact the Universe: it would be quite foreign and incomprehensible to him. But, as esoteric development proceeds, man finds that he can contact and understand the Universe more and more, because he is linked indissolubly with it *interiorly*.

To conclude this chapter on levels of being, there is a very important phrase in The Work to the effect that: *our level of being attracts our life*. This statement is well worthy of consideration here. Ordinarily, people think that if only they had better opportunities for self-expression, or had been born in different circumstances, or had had better chances in life, etc., then they would be different people living in an entirely different type of environment, with everything going according to how they wanted it to go. But The Work phrase just quoted shows clearly that the only way in which we can change external circumstances or conditions is by changing ourselves *within*. It is what we are within that dictates what our environment and external conditions of living shall be, strange as this may seem to most people. People are so used to thinking that the way to change oneself is to try to change externals, first, that the esoteric viewpoint is very hard for them to appreciate, let alone accept. Yet, everything points to its validity, if only we study other people and ourselves carefully.

A person who is discontented with his or her life, for instance, thinks that if only they could go abroad, say, or get a different type of job, or have a different circle of friends, or whatever else of an external nature of this sort it may be, then they could be different people and live life far more happily. But even if they succeed in doing any of these things, they find to their dismay that the same set of life-happenings seems to dog their footsteps, no matter how vainly they seek to alter them by the external changes they may make. *And this is because their level of being has not changed;* so that, no matter what external changes they seek to bring about, life for them follows in essentials the same pattern. It is only when the level of being alters that any real change can be effected in the outward circumstances of life, because it must take place in step with the changes within. This is an esoteric law which can explain much to those capable of noting its real significance.

For instance, it does away at once with all the restlessness characteristic of most people today. They are so dissatisfied with life that they are continually seeking for ways in which to change their lives externally; but once they realise that it is only by changing themselves from within—through work on themselves—that any change can be effected in their outer lives, then they begin to become different people. They no longer have the restless urge for change, and are contented to be as they are, because they realize that it is through what takes place *within them* that anything can be expected to alter for the good in their environment.

Nothing *spectacular* can be expected, in this direction, but as we proceed to work on ourselves, and our level of being changes accordingly, so we begin to find that life's pattern begins to change, too, so that we are no longer confronted by a series of daily happenings of the old familiar kind. The pattern changes in conformity with the inner change, so that we gradually emerge into an entirely different kind of life, although superficially living just as heretofore. The casual observer would note very little difference, perhaps, but we ourselves can tell without any difficulty that things are becoming different. This is exactly as it should be, because our external life is the school in which we have to learn our lessons in living, so that the lessons will automatically change as we change.

CHAPTER XIII

METANOIA

THE Greek word *metanoia* is perhaps used more than any other in the five volumes which comprise Dr. Nicoll's *Commentaries*. As translated in the Bible the word is taken to mean *repentance,* but according to Dr. Nicoll this is quite wrong, its true meaning being *change of mind.* Before one can embark on the quest for Self-Knowledge one has to have a completely different mental attitude both to oneself and the world in which one lives, and to the Universe in general; and that change of mental outlook is exactly what is implied in the Greek word *metanoia.* To infer that this word means repentance, as in a religious aspect, is to give to it a completely erroneous connotation. The aspirant towards a more spiritual way of life will be thrown entirely off the scent. To attain "Life eternal" we do not have to "repent of our sins". Metanoia does not imply repenting, nor has it anything to do with sinning, as such. It means a completely different orientation of oneself to oneself and all that has hitherto taken up one's interests, desires, views about the future, and so forth. This new mental outlook is precisely what is implied by the word metanoia as found in the Greek version of the New Testament, and erroneously translated in the Authorized Version as repentance.

In the ordinary course of events people are continually "changing their minds", but that is not in the least what is implied by the use of the term in the present context. *We have to begin to think in a new way;* a way hitherto quite unknown to us. We have to stop thinking in the old way, and begin to use our minds quite differently. The steps required for this mental transformation of ourselves are very clearly defined in the esoteric system we are discussing. *This mental transformation is the essential pre-requisite for that change of being which is the basis of Self-Knowledge; and it is most important for the reader to realise this fact.* In the past he has been accustomed to reading about this and that subject and adding to his already existing stock of ideas, so that it has gradually grown over the years and presents a body of knowledge which—in general—is the basis from which his thoughts and actions proceed.

We must allow for the pressure of subconscious and other irrational factors which lead us often into action against our more conscious wishes and desires; but in general it is the gradually accumulating body of knowledge, based on study, experience, etc., which is what we may regard as the furniture of our minds. Everything we come into contact with, whether a new system of philosophy, or any new idea of any kind whatsoever, or any new experience, etc., is always referred automatically to the mental furniture with which our minds are stocked, or, better, encumbered. *We cannot possibly take in anything really new,* because it has to be sorted out and made to fit in with what the mind already possesses. The result is that any essential "newness" is immediately filtered out and lost. It is extremely difficult for people generally to realize this most important fact, but it *is* a fact, and explains why so few people are able to profit from the thoughts and writings of men such as Gurdjieff, Ouspensky and Krishnamurti.

The thoughts and ideas of such individuals do not seem to connect up with what we already have in our minds, and so our first impulse is to reject them. Some people even go so far as to say such "higher thoughts" are quite incomprehensible. Thus they show quite clearly that, as far as their own minds are concerned, the higher thoughts contain nothing which corresponds to anything the person concerned has already in his mind. He finds nothing on which he can grip, nothing with which he can feel at home in his own thought world. That is why new teachings of any kind—really new teachings—have such a very hard time to find people ready to receive them. One must have the mental capacity and ability to be able to recognize them as new, and not expect them to conform to or be in harmony with what one already knows. All of which is extremely difficult—if not impossible—for most Western people. Their minds function in a certain pattern and so nothing which does not connect in some way with this pattern is acceptable to them.

This does not mean to say that such minds are not responsive to new ideas, as such. They usually are responsive to all kinds, but such ideas are not new in the sense of being *fundamentally* new. They are only new superficially, and have something in them which already corresponds to the habitual mental outlook and way of thinking of the recipient. That is why metanoia is so entirely different, and means so much when used by Dr. Nicoll in his *Commentaries*. It indicates a clean break with all that has gone before in mental thought and activity; the bringing into being of something entirely different in one's thought-life. It means *thinking in a new way, thinking on a new level*.

The previously uninformed reader may feel like asking at this juncture : how, then, can I acquire this new method of thinking, having regard to all that you have been saying in the present chapter? In reply to this most pertinent question we can say quite definitely that the attainment of metanoia *IS NOT SOMETHING WHICH IS OPEN TO ALL AND SUNDRY*. Only certain people are capable of achieving it; those people possessed of *magnetic centre*, about which we have already spoken. Lest any reader should feel discouraged by this statement, let him or her be assured that they would

hardly have read thus far unless they had already some
development of magnetic centre. How is it to be done? It is
precisely here that The Work makes its greatest contribution.
Every phase of The Work is in a sense an aspect of metanoia,
because it demands a complete reversal of ordinary thinking.
Before The Work can do this for us, however, *our minds must
be in such a condition as to make it possible for such a change
of thinking to be effected.* Therefore, the achievement of
metanoia may be said to be a two-way process. We must be
capable first of all of thinking in a new way; and then, if we
are so capable, The Work teachings will show us how this can
be accomplished. It is essentially a self-appointed task. No
one can coerce or force us into it. It is something which must
come essentially from ourselves, as a result of our own
conscious volition.

Although we cannot go into the subject more fully, we can
say that one of the chief avenues made available by The Work
for the achievement of metanoia is *receiving and registering
impressions in a new way.* The Work posits three different
kinds of food as necessary for man, these three being ordinary
food, air, and impressions. We are all accustomed to the idea
of food as being essential to life, also air, for without breathing
we should be dead in a few minutes. But extremely few
people would ever imagine that impressions are even more
important to us than food and air. But such is so, according
to The Work. *It is said that if all sense impressions were cut
off from us for even a few seconds we would not be able to
live.* We are accustomed to the constant stream of impressions we receive via our senses, and this teaching about their
immense importance is of the greatest value to us as well as
interest, for, as we have said, it is by beginning to register
impressions *differently* that we can begin to achieve metanoia
for ourselves.

Ordinarily, we allow all impressions to fall on what may
be called "the associative network" in our minds. By which

we mean the associative background of thoughts and ideas which has been built up and developed from birth onwards, in accordance with our upbringing, education, and so forth. The associative network receives every impression that comes to us via our senses, according to a set pattern—developed over the years—which pattern may be said to be our distinct and personal "note"—it is *us*, i.e., that which distinguishes us from other people and gives us our distinctive tone or key. Therefore, to transform ourselves (to achieve metanoia, that is) we must begin to receive impressions *differently*. That is one of the secrets which The Work makes clear to us in regard to this all-important problem. The fact that this is *possible* is *in itself* of the profoundest significance, for it means that we really *can* become *different people* eventually. Just think what that means to people who have an understanding of what is *really* their *present* position. It is indeed a message of the greatest hope. It means that we no longer have to take life, ourselves and the Universe in exactly the same way as here-tofore. By receiving and registering impressions differently, we change everything within and around us. *This is so because, fundamentally, everything—including ourselves—is merely impressions conveyed to us by our senses.*

Everyone will agree that if a number of people are exposed to the same experience they will all register in a different way. To some it will appear in a certain light, to others in a different light, all according to their distinctive associative net-work pattern, which has been explained. It is well known that if you ask people to describe any incident which they have all witnessed, they will tend to give conflicting views about it, and this is so precisely for the reason just given. Their associative network will filter-out the incident *according to their own particular key,* and the result will be something essentially different for each person concerned, although all have partaken of the same experience. Therefore, to be able to receive impressions in a new way, as The Work teaches, we have to be able to put a brake on the mechanical manner in which our impressions are acted upon by the associative network in our minds. This action continues quite mechanically all the time, and entirely without our conscious choice or volition. We have, therefore, to bring *consciousness* into the equation, something which by far the great majority of people think they already do, but which they very surely do not. They do this because the whole manner of ordinary living implies that what we do habitually is entirely mechanical, the result of the functioning of the associative network pattern within us, which sorts out all our impressions for us according to its own working, without our having any conscious control over the operation. We *think* we are in control, and that we do everything consciously, but that is merely one of the gigantic illusions which ordinary life imposes on us, and which keeps us enchained to it. To free ourselves from the grip of ordinary life is—in one sense—the chief aim of The Work, because until we can become free we are quite incapable of even attempting to carry out The Work teachings, which, in turn, means we are incapable of achieving metanoia.

Thus, the whole question of the attainment of metanoia revolves around receiving and registering impressions in a new way. In his *Commentaries* Dr. Nicoll gives countless illustrations of how this can be (and must be) done. The first step is to try to create as it were a breathing space between the reception of impressions and their further development, according to the working of the associative network pattern which is our key. That is to say, instead of allowing our impressions (brought to us by our senses) to be dealt with according to the manner which has previously been the habitual pattern, we have to try to step in consciously and prevent this automatic reaction. We have to allow the impressions a chance to be received by our minds differently, *not* as heretofore. As just said, the first step towards this achievement is to try to create a space between the incoming impressions and the receptive associative network. The more we can succeed in creating this space (through *conscious* effort) the more room will there be for the impressions to be received differently and acted upon differently. This is by no means an easy thing to accomplish; nothing of real esoteric value ever is easy to attain. The more we work on ourselves in accordance with The Work teachings, however, the more possibility will there be for impressions to be received differently, with results quite different from those previously secured. It is these different results which form the basis of that mental transformation which metanoia implies.

There is much talk in The Work about the transformation of energies (termed hydrogens). This is a very complicated subject, and we do not propose to go into the matter. We refer to the subject here merely because it is the transformation of impressions (under the aegis of metanoia) which produces the transformation of energies within us which makes esoteric development possible. This is a subject about which the orthodox scientist knows nothing, and it opens up an entirely new mode of thinking about ourselves and our interior workings. Nothing in Nature works without its appropriate energy. If we wish to attain Self-Knowledge, the energies requisite for the task must be forthcoming from somewhere. We begin to secure the necessary energies through metanoia via the initial step of beginning to receive and register impressions in a new way. Thus, each aspect of The Work is bound up with its every other aspect, to form one all-embracing whole. One cannot hope to know all about every aspect at once, but as the years pass one becomes aware of more and more of the teachings in application to one's own daily life, and that is the only way The Work can really be absorbed. It is essentially something which must become part of our daily lives, and be worked out in and through them. It is *not* something apart from daily life, to be read about and thought about, but never incorporated into our daily scheme of living. We hope that what we have said about *metanoia* will give the reader a satisfactory, if not complete, idea of its significance in The Work scheme as a whole, and of its essential practicality. Before we leave the subject of metanoia, it will be interesting for the reader to note that from the angle of The Work four different levels of thinking are indicated. These are: (1) *Alogical thinking;* (2) *Logical thinking;* (3) *Psychological thinking;* and (4) *Greater Mind.* Alogical thinking is that very primitive type of thinking which is based largely on superstition, suggestion, etc.

Logical thinking is the everyday type of thinking which is based on what the senses bring to us and thereafter elaborated by the processes of rational thought.

Psychological thinking is the new type of thinking which metanoia implies, whereby and wherein one sees the *inner* meaning, significance, and relationship of things, and is not bound by what the senses and logical thought indicate. It is thinking beyond the confines of the ordinary everyday mind.

Greater Mind is the realm or plane whereon Cosmic Ideation exists and operates. It is the source from which all creation derives, and is implicit in the phrase "the unseen is the cause of the seen". That is to say, unless and until a thing has been envisaged in the realm of Greater Mind it can have no finite existence, whether it be a Solar System or a rabbit. Everything originates in Greater Mind. Unless one believes in its existence, one can never be in a position to adopt the esoteric way of life. Such a way of life presupposes the existence of Greater Mind, and is based directly upon it.

The teaching of The Work about the four different levels of thinking has great significance for the esoteric student, and shows once again how far more revealing and deep-rooted are the basic truths of Esotericism than those now current in the Western World.

Note on Imagination :

We feel we should say something here about imagination in relation to The Work. According to the system we are discussing *the wrong use of imagination* is at the root of most of our troubles. It is common in our mental and emotional life, and affects almost our every thought and feeling. The ramifications of the wrong use of imagination have to be fully realized before we can hope to control it. Therefore, much of The Work teaching is directed to that very end, in a variety of different ways, some of which have already been spoken about, but from somewhat different angles. On the other hand, *the right use of imagination* is something which The Work wishes to encourage as much as possible. Imagination, when used correctly, for creative and positive ends, is the most potent force we can employ in our aim of esoteric development. There is no limit to what creative imagination can achieve for us, just as there is no limit to what the wrong use of imagination will produce in bringing about our undoing. In the vital issue between the right and wrong use of our power of imagination lies, in one sense, the chief battleground for work on ourselves. All The Work teachings are designed to aid us in our self-appointed task : for it is essentially a task which we ourselves can accomplish and must accomplish. No one else can do it for us.

CHAPTER XIV

THE FOUR STATES OF CONSCIOUSNESS

A VITAL teaching of The Work is that about the four states of consciousness, which now we propose to discuss.

In the ordinary way we are aware of only two states of consciousness : (1) when we are asleep; and (2) when we are awake. Indeed, the former is not regarded as a state of consciousness, and so we look upon being wakeful as our only state of consciousness. We regard ourselves as being fully conscious then, and modern psychology supports that viewpoint. In The Work, however, four states of consciousness are posited. (1) the State of Sleep; (2) the ordinary Waking State; (3) the State of Self-Remembering; and (4) the State of Objective Consciousness.

The interesting point about this fourfold division of consciousness is that it regards man's ordinary waking state (wherein he is considered to be fully conscious) as a state of partial sleep, i.e., a state wherein man is not fully awake, because he could not live the life of mechanical response and reaction to events which characterizes it if he were fully awake. It is on this very issue that The Work throws out its greatest challenge to everyday thinking. What is ordinarily considered to be full consciousness, The Work regards as a form of waking sleep, wherein we do everything mechanically and without real conscious thought. Of course, we are convinced that we *are* fully conscious, and that we direct our lives in their every detail; but that is only another of the gigantic illusions under which ordinary life compels us to live, to keep us within its thrall. *The more fully we believe what life seems to tell us, the more completely are we its slaves, its willing slaves.*

It is most important for the reader to realize this fact, because, so long as we allow life to lure us on with its offers of what seem rewards for ambition, self-interest, greed, lust, and all the other urges and desires of the personality seeking fulfilment, just so long do we remain the slave of life, bound hand and foot to it and by it. According to the Evolutionary Scheme under which man lives on earth, it is sufficient for the purposes of ordinary life that he should remain as he is, under the sway of the personality, and eager for the prizes which life seems to offer to those who compete for its favours in the hurly-burly of everyday existence. While man is thus immersed in life he has no thought or desire for anything higher. Therefore, for the purposes of Esotericism the sleep of the potentially higher within him must be awakened, otherwise he will remain forever in the state in which he now is, glued to life and its ever-willing dupe. It is for this reason that in The Work man's present wakeful state is regarded as a form of *sleep,* because in it he is asleep to what is higher within him, or rather to what is potentially higher within him. Only his awakening to a knowledge of this all-important fact can make it possible for the higher part of himself to develop. *Man asleep* is a common phrase of The Work for man as he is in ordinary waking consciousness. The more he remains glued to life with all its enchantments, so-called, the more he is assumed to be asleep. Therefore a mighty effort at awakening is required before any of us can attempt the climb to those peaks within us which Esotericism demands, and which Esotericism will show us how to attain.

The first of the steps in inner development is what The Work calls *the state of Self-Remembering* (already referred to in Chapter V). In this condition the seeker after self-knowledge is no longer in the grip of life but in the process of being freed from its all-embracing clutches. He is becoming conscious of his real destiny as an evolving spiritual being, and is no longer in the state of waking sleep which formerly characterized his condition when he identified himself completely with his personality. He is now in a position to know the personality for what it really is, and to regard himself as a far greater and more sublime being in every way, because he is now resident in that part of himself which is his REAL SELF. At first—under the aegis of The Work—the state of Self-Remembering can be achieved only for very brief periods, but as we progress inwards towards what is most real in us the state of Self-Remembering becomes of increasingly longer duration. In time, it becomes a permanent state (achieved by very few mortals, but nevertheless still a possibility). The fourth state of consciousness The Work speaks about, i.e., *Objective Consciousness* is the state in which the individual is able to take in everything in the Cosmos as it *really is,* stripped of all the illusions in which our everyday senses enwrap us in our contacts with the Universe. We see things as they really are, and knowledge is directly apprehended in every field to which we turn. This fourth state of consciousness is, therefore, outside the scope of ordinary man. *It is the state in which REAL I lives,* in touch with the eternal verities.

The fourfold division of consciousness has therefore great significance. The more we study it, the more does it open to us doors of understanding. It shows how vastly superior the psychology of Esotericism is to that of ordinary psychology, with its assumption that so long as we are awake we are fully conscious. *Full consciousness* is something reserved for extremely few mortals, and the sooner we ordinary beings become aware of the fact, the better will it be for us in every way. It will tend to instil into us some well-needed humility, which is most essential if we wish to climb the ladder of esoteric development which leads both inwards and upwards at the same time. When man can regard his everyday waking life as a state of sleep, wherein his dormant spiritual faculties are encased in layer upon layer of insulating material which shuts them off effectually from any whisper of what *might be,* then he is in a position to *begin to wake up,* which is the prerequisite for actually becoming awake. In other words, before we can wake up we have to become aware of the necessity for doing so. While man thinks he is already awake it is obvious that the much-needed awakening which Esotericism requires will never be forthcoming. Hence the insistence in all The Work teachings that *man is asleep,* in which state he is a mere automaton, an automaton which, none the less, can make war, write books, fall in love, create empires, and do all those things which people regard as the fruits of being fully awake.

CHAPTER XV

Man and the Cosmos

Most people have no philosophy of life. They merely drift through life without any real understanding of the why or wherefore of their existence. If they are orthodoxly religious, their religion can be regarded as their philosophy of life; but in most cases it does not seem to have any marked impact upon either their consciousness or their behaviour. Others turn to political creeds or ideologies for a philosophy of life, deeming the religious way bereft of any meaning or significance for them; while others quite frankly do not bother about the matter at all, and merely live their lives on a day-to-day basis without thought of any inner meaning or significance being attached to whatever they may or may not do. When one comes into touch with Esotericism, however, one realises that a philosophy of life is not only essential, but the basis upon which everything else rests. Without a philosophy in which man is regarded as an essential part of the Cosmos, directly related to it in every detail, and incapable of living his life fully without knowing what exactly is his own part in the great Cosmic Plan, Esotericism as such would be an impossibility, and even an absurdity. It rests essentially upon the acceptance of the fact that man and the Cosmos are inseparable, and that each derives its significance from something which binds them both together. That "something" is the GREAT EVOLUTIONARY PLAN OF CREATION of which the Universe and all that it contains is the expression.

Without that Creative Power and Plan behind it the Universe and man would both be quite meaningless and pointless.

There are many people, e.g., Materialists, who regard both the Universe and man as being pointless and purposeless; but that is precisely because they are incapable of seeing anything behind material manifestation, and regard everything as being the result of mere chance or accident. How mind, intelligence, and spiritual powers and potentialities can be the outcome of mere chance or accident, materialists do not seem to be able to explain. That does not, however, prevent them from going on saying that everything *is* quite meaningless and the outcome of mere chance or accident. That this viewpoint is very common and popular nowadays is most unfortunate, because it robs people of any real incentive for living. The substitution of a political creed for such an incentive can do nothing to restore the situation; for it is looking to externals to replace something which should essentially spring from within ourselves.

When people come into touch with The Work they find at once that man's relationship with the Cosmos is taken as the basis of everything. Without it The Work could not exist. It derives its significance from the fact that only through its agency man can come more fully into relationship with the powers which direct the evolution of the Universe in which we live and move and have our being, and make that relationship increasingly fruitful as time passes.

Once we begin to realize that the inner core of ourselves is directly related to the creative power which has brought the Universe into existence—which is what The Work and Esotericism posit—then everything takes on a different meaning. We find meaning and purpose everywhere, in everything we see, hear, think, say and do. Where before we saw only vaguely, now we begin to see things more clearly as we tread the esoteric path. We no longer flounder about in life, not knowing what it all means and being quite unaware of our own place in the daily scheme of things; we now know what is our own individual rôle. The more we try to live it, the more do we become aware of the fact that we and the Universe are one, and that our destiny is indissolubly linked with it, in a sense no material understanding of things can bring.

The trouble with a great many people today—owing to the growth of science—is that they will believe only what their senses tell them or show them. They believe that anything which cannot be seen, heard, weighed, measured or touched or smelled has no real existence. Therefore—even though many such people are professedly religious in the orthodox sense—they refuse to believe in anything which science tells them is outside its scope or realm. They appear to believe that unless and until a thing is amenable to the practices of the scientific method it cannot possibly be *real*. In reality, anything which science can tell us about the Universe and ourselves is essentially *unreal*, because it is merely the result of sense-data. Anything which the senses reveal of the Universe must inevitably be false or unreal, because it is an extraction from what that reality is through the medium of the very senses which make us aware of it. In other words, whatever our senses (and the scientific instruments based on them) reveal to us, must inevitably be a modification of the basic reality, because our senses cannot possibly contact reality direct. By their very nature they are quite incapable of any such thing.

Therefore, in regarding what science reveals to us of the Universe as being *real*, and everything beyond scientific computation or analysis as being therefore *unreal*, twentieth-century man makes the biggest mistake possible in his assessment of both the Cosmos and himself. That is why when one comes into touch with Esotericism, through any of its channels, an entirely different approach to reality is opened up. We begin to realise that the *unseen* is always the cause of the *seen,* and must forever be so; and to look for proof about things spiritual through the scientific method is not only an impossibility, but an absurdity.

Every esoteric system has its own ways of showing man's relationship to the Cosmos and the "inner realms" as they may be called. In The Work there are quite a number of important charts and diagrams connected with this all-important subject. They show how man came into existence —as part of the great evolutionary plan of creation—and how he is linked with worlds and spheres both higher and lower than himself. Without a knowledge of this relationship it would not be possible to apply The Work teachings intelligently and with definite purpose. One would be going on one's way quite blindly, as it were. Therefore, such knowledge is always available for those desirous of treading the esoteric path, once they have felt themselves drawn to it. It is an essential feature of the whole process of inner development, as already intimated. Old esoteric sayings such as : "as above, so below", and "the Macrocosm and the Microcosm", point the way to an understanding of how the inner relationship between man and the Cosmos has been known in esoteric circles right down through the ages, and has been passed on from generation to generation among the initiated.

In Dr. Nicoll's *Commentaries,* and in Ouspensky's *In Search of the Miraculous* all the charts and diagrams dealing with the subject under discussion will be found, including the most mysterious and enigmatic one of all, *The Enneagram.* To these books the reader is referred for a detailed study of the subject. The point about this teaching of The Work anent Man and the Cosmos, which affects us—as individuals—most strongly, is that a sharp distinction is made between man *as he is* and man *as he might be.* It is explained that as he is, man is a creature designed to further the purposes of Life or Nature, and to fit into a certain niche in the evolutionary scheme. At that level, and for that purpose, man is essentially a puppet in life's power, and he fulfils a function and purpose which life wants him to fulfil.

To that end man is kept asleep (in The Work sense) and whatever he does is done mechanically and under the direct hypnosis of life, even though man may consider himself to be fully conscious and fully aware of whatever he is doing, and wants to do. All of which is, of course, due to the hypnosis under which man lives, and is part of the plan of his existence as a slave of life. That is man's present position. It is only when he becomes aware of his position that there is any possibility of his waking up and becoming something different. Only Esotericism can make him become something different, and so fulfil *a higher plan in the great cosmic design*, a design about which man as he now is knows nothing and can know nothing. It is this most significant and vitally important truth which Esotericism (and The Work) makes clear to us, via the diagrams and charts to which we have referred.

One of The Work diagrams (known as *The Ray of Creation*) shows the relationship of Earth to the rest of the Universe, down from *The Absolute*, through *All Possible Worlds* to *The Galaxy, The Sun, Planets, Earth* and *Moon*. Another, known as *The Side Octave From The Sun*, shows man's relationship—as part of organic life—with the Solar System. With the aid of these two diagrams one is able to see the part that man plays in the cosmic scheme; the point being that, *as he is*, man is an unfinished product serving the ends of Life and Nature, as just briefly indicated, but also showing *what he could do*, with the aid of Esotericism. Man as he now is lives under certain categories of Cosmic Law, which keep him at his present level of development. Once he begins to work on himself, under the aegis of The Work teachings, he begins to put himself under different categories of Cosmic Law. These Laws operate at a higher level than the laws under which man lives ordinarily. They can only come into operation in his life when man realises his present position as the slave of life, and wishes to alter his status and become a more conscious being, working in conscious harmony with the higher Cosmic Laws that are ready to operate on his behalf as soon as he puts himself under their influence. It is precisely the same with a seed, for example. While it is out of the ground the seed exists under certain Cosmic Laws, and under these laws it remains a seed and can be nothing else. As soon as it is planted in the soil and given water and air and sunshine, it becomes an entirely different thing. It ceases to be a seed and begins to become a plant, something which was impossible until it was placed in a suitable environment.

Exactly the same with man. While he remains at his present level, man lives his life under certain categories of natural law, but, like the seed out of the ground, he cannot go beyond a certain limited stage. When he realizes his true position and begins to try to ascend the evolutionary ladder *through self-directed effort* (via The Work) he comes automatically under the direction of the higher range of laws to which we have referred. His life henceforth becomes something entirely different from what it was previously. The analogy between the seed out of the ground and the seed in the ground is exactly applicable to man. Just as the seed's destiny is entirely different in each situation, being under entirely different categories of Cosmic Law, so is man's destiny entirely different if he begins to work on himself under the impact of Esotericism. Laws then come into operation which could not possibly affect him previously, and the result is that an entirely new level of being can be achieved, a level entirely beyond the scope of everyday man to conceive. Outwardly, there may be no apparent difference, but inwardly there is every possible difference. This is not something which man can achieve in one jump, as it were; it is a gradual process taking many years to accomplish. Once one's foot is upon the Esoteric Path the limitations which ring man in at his everyday level are shaken off. New vistas are opened up which far transcend anything the everyday mind can comprehend. As we have said, there is no sudden metamorphosis. One's destiny takes on a new dimension, because of the new understanding of man's real relationship with the Cosmos that The Work teachings upon this vitally important subject bring to one.

We referred just now to one of The Work diagrams about *The Side Octave From The Sun*. The word octave comes very frequently into The Work teachings, because it is realized that *the octave* is a definite universal scale, which has its ramifications in all sorts of conditions and factors affecting both the Cosmos and Man. The musical scale of seven notes embraced in an octave is a symbol of the part that the number *seven* plays in all manifestation, from the highest cosmic levels down to the lowest, and so, the octave or musical scale is used very frequently to bring out certain significances and teachings of The Work. The most important aspect of the use of the octave (or musical scale) in relationship to man, is the fact that at two points in the scale—when the scale is taken as representing man's inner development—certain "shocks" have to be administered, in order to make it possible for man to pass from the note achieved to the next-higher note. This is a very important teaching, and most significant. It shows a profound understanding of the inner working of the Cosmos generally; because every phase of cosmic development—including that of the Cosmos itself—is subject to this law about "shocks". What the shocks are, and how administered, must be left to the reader to discover on more intensive study of The Work literature, to which this book is merely a brief introduction.

We also referred just now to a diagram about *The Ray of Creation*. The important point to note is that this particular ray of creation is only one of millions radiating in all directions from *The Absolute*. It has special significance for us because our Sun and Earth are on this particular ray, whereas myriads of other Suns and Earths are on other similar rays.

Many people assume that life exists only on our Earth and nowhere else in the Universe. This is fallacious, as a study of esoteric teachings soon makes clear. Life is everywhere, infilling every particle of space, and manifesting itself in countless different forms, according to the matter and conditions of the part of the Universe wherein it is located. The matter through which life expresses itself on the material level is constantly breaking down and renewing itself all over the Universe, as modern astronomers are beginning to realise. Instead of space being a vacuum, it is the breeding-ground for ever newer material aggregations, acting under the impetus of the life manifesting through such aggregations. The vast panorama of teeming Life and Creation opened up to us through the teachings of Esotericism beggars human thought. It gives us a better perspective of the real worth of scientific discoveries up to date, when taken on a *cosmic* scale.

Another very important teaching in regard to the subject-matter of the present chapter is that Evolution itself could never be possible without a prior *Involution*. By this is meant that evolution of spirit through material forms could never take place without a prior involution of spirit into matter. Spirit comes down from *The Absolute* and clothes itself in increasingly denser forms of materiality in order to further the work of cosmic creation (*The Ray of Creation* being a representation of this process). When spirit has reached its lowest point, it begins the return journey upwards, which is termed Evolution. Without the prior descent of spirit into matter for the purposes of cosmic creation, on the material level, the return could not possibly take place. Evolution as understood by modern science is a most limited conception. It is regarded as merely an evolution of form without any spiritual connotation whatsoever. Even when viewed as a process of inner spiritual development through forms of ever-increasing material complexity, through the amoeba, plant, insect, reptile, animal, to man, it is still a partial understanding of the process, as we hope the reader can now realize. This subject is one which all Eastern religious and philosophical systems thoroughly understand.

The foregoing brief references to The Work teachings . 'ut the Universe and man open up to us a vast cosmic canvas upon which is depicted ideas and concepts transcending anything available to current Western thinking. They enlarge our scope of mental understanding to an extent, and to a degree, with which nothing in Western thought can compare. Not only so, they give a lift and buoyancy to man's spirit which in itself is of the greatest possible value to him. These teachings make it abundantly clear that man is an essential factor in Universal development, working on a reciprocal basis with the Cosmos itself, *provided he really is aware of his special place in the Cosmic Scheme, and knows how to make use of that knowledge to further his own spiritual destiny.*

At present that destiny is hidden from the vast majority of people, with the result that they lead completely aimless lives which, although they may bring some reward in material happiness and satisfaction of a temporary nature, can never be of a completely satisfying character. Man feels he is missing "something" to complete his happiness in living; but what that "something" is, he is quite unable to discover, unless and until he is brought into touch with Esotericism in one of its many forms. Then he will begin to observe what has been missing in his life, rendering that life barren, despite "triumphs" in the material world. In short, unless man starts out to discover what is his real relationship to the Cosmos, as explained in Esoteric teaching, he is an orphan wandering around aimlessly in a world which is completely alien to him, and must forever be alien to him. When Knowledge is at last forthcoming, everything is changed immediately. Man is no longer a stranger crying in the wilderness; he is *at home* in a world which has real meaning and significance for him.

The feeling of "at-homeness" does not come right away.

At first it is only a mental concept arising out of one's study
of the ideas and thoughts that we have outlined very briefly.
In time, however, a definite emotional feeling begins to arise
whereby one feels increasingly attuned to the Cosmos. This
feeling continues to develop as the process of *work on oneself*
—in accordance with The Work teachings—progresses. It is
impossible to compare the inner state of someone in this
situation with that of someone living in the everyday world of
today, who has no inkling of esoteric teachings, no matter
how exalted he may be, either philosophically, aesthetically,
artistically, or scientifically. Such a man is living essentially
on the *outside* of things; whereas a person who is treading the
esoteric path in accordance with The Work teachings is
definitely on the *inside* of things. Hence the vast difference in
the feelings of such people, both towards themselves and the
Cosmos in general.

We have not dealt with *all* the various facets of The Work
teachings regarding the relationship of man to the Cosmos in
the present chapter. We have merely alluded briefly to some
of them. If the reader's interest has been whetted he can study
the subject more comprehensively by referring to the works
of Ouspensky and Dr. Nicoll which we have already mentioned. It has been our purpose to just introduce the subject,
in order to show how vast and all-embracing are the cosmic
conceptions which The Work has to put before the minds of
those who appreciate what they are receiving, and who give
thanks accordingly in all humility.

We cannot conclude the present chapter, however, without
referring to what The Work says about good and evil. The
Work maintains that everything which leads man *upwards*
towards his spiritual goal is good, and everything that leads
him *downwards, away from that goal,* is evil. This cuts directly
away from the usual philosophical wrangling about this all-
important subject. We have already said that there is a down-
ward process in operation in the Universe, from spirit into

increasingly concrete forms of matter (*Involution*), and an upward process leading from the lowest forms of manifested life towards higher and higher degrees of consciousness and spiritual awakening (*Evolution*). These two processes are continuous throughout the vast confines of the Universe. Therefore, anything which helps on the evolutionary process is deemed good, and anything which impedes it is deemed evil. This all links up with man's ultimate destiny, which is to become a progressively more *conscious being* and willing co-worker with the Universal Creative Power which has brought him—and all Life—into existence, in fulfilment of the great creative scheme of which the Universe is the expression.

According to Esotericism the Universe was created in the first place to give expression to the creative urge of The Absolute in its dual aspect of spirit (or consciousness) and matter, and man—as part of creation—is one aspect of the process. His parentage is divine because he springs from THAT WHICH HAS BROUGHT ALL INTO EXISTENCE, and ultimately he will rejoin that Divinity which is his progenitor. It is a thought of tremendous impact to realize what all this means, and to appreciate that within himself man bears the seed of his own divinity. A staggering and also sobering thought is that everything that can lead man towards this ultimate fulfilment is *good,* because it is assisting the Divine Plan; and everything which leads man away from the fulfilment of this divine destiny is *evil or bad.* Good and evil regarded in the foregoing light may have little or nothing to do with ethical or moral judgments based on current conceptions, and in The Work this distinction is clearly drawn. It is stated that as man is today, living in his personality, under the aegis of custom, tradition, orthodox religion, etc., that which guides him in regard to good and evil is *acquired conscience,* which is the product of the forces and factors to which we have referred. But when man really begins to work on himself, and treads the esoteric path, *real conscience* begins to emerge. It is this which unerringly tells us whether what we are doing is good or evil in the esoteric (or cosmic) sense. Acquired conscience can be different as between one country and another, and as between one century and another; it is something which shifts and changes all the time. But *real* conscience is always the same and never changes, because it is rooted in that which is changeless and everlasting.

Thus, the more man moves along the path to his inner un-folding, and thereby gradually achieves his true destiny, the more will he come under the aegis of the real or buried conscience which is the voice of the Divine within him, and his true guide along the path of return towards his destined goal, which was also his point of origin. The movement out-wards into manifestation presupposes the movement back-ward again into real spirit (or consciousness), of which REAL "I" is the symbol for all those engaged in The Work.

It will be observed that man must become a *willing* co-operator with the Creative Power behind the Universe if he is to achieve his real destiny, once he realises what that destiny is, as revealed by Esotericism. The emergence of *Real Will* is therefore a very important factor to be noted.

Man must exercise his *will* to become more conscious, in fulfilment of his aim. Such use of the will is far different from what ordinarily passes for resolution in the everyday world. We who live in the personality regard will as merely the strongest of the conflicting desires which may be in existence at any one time. The strongest desire wins a temporary mastery, and that is what we regard as will. It is a purely transitory phenomenon, however, and is soon replaced by another desire which gains temporary predominance according to the circumstances of the moment.

In the sense of our discussion Will is something entirely different. It is the result of conscious realisation of what is required if one is to begin to fulfil one's true cosmic destiny.

It is therefore something compounded of both consciousness and inner purpose, allied to inflexible determination. Such will is the very essence of a man's feeling, and springs from the very core of himself. The development of real will could, in one sense, be the sole purpose of The Work, for it embodies all that is implied in the phrase: *work on oneself*. One works on oneself in order to develop the necessary will-power to carry one on the task of achieving more consciousness for oneself, in order, thereby, to fulfil more ably one's aims of inner unfoldment.

That aim is not one which implies an orderly progression from *what one is* to *what one is destined to be*. There are numerous different obstacles to be overcome on the way. One is continually falling back under the pull of the personality and its host of "I's" who are opposed to The Work and all for which it stands. As soon as one feels he is making headway, the opposition is roused to battle within one, causing some of the ground that has been gained to be lost; and so the struggle persists, swaying one way and then the other, with never any clear-cut progression towards one's goal. Progress is made, nevertheless, not only despite, but actually because of, the conflict which is continually going on within one as one seeks to obey the urge to Self-Realization which The Work indicates and makes possible.

Finally, after putting forth the foregoing few basic ideas regarding The Work teachings, we feel it is most important to stress the fact that the Universe is a symbol of *unity in diversity*. By this is meant that everything in the Universe is the expression of the one Creative Power manifested in material form, so that no matter how prodigious the apparent diversity of such forms, they all have one underlying unity. The Universe *is one organic whole,* no matter how diverse and widely differing its manifold aspects may seem to be. This is a truth of the most fundamental importance which Esotericism has promulgated throughout the ages, but which modern science is still far from realizing. To the modern mind in general there is bewildering diversity everywhere, and no unifying principle, but instead an inner feeling of separateness from everything.

The more one delves beneath the surface, however, the more does the existence of an underlying unity begin to reveal itself, and then one feels oneness and kinship with everything that is. One realizes that all springs from the same common source and all is merely the outward expression of its restless creative power. This creative power expresses itself in and through everything. All its laws operate in and through everything, too. We do not stand outside, as it were, and observe those laws in operation; they are at work in us. We and everything else are subject to their sway, as symbols of the ONE CREATIVE ENERGY which brought them and us into existence.

CHAPTER XVI

THE LIMITATIONS OF LOGICAL THINKING

MOST of what we have said up to now has had reference mainly to the Gurdjieff system, with not much actual reference to the teachings of Krishnamurti, although much of what has been said will be found to be applicable to both systems of teaching (if Krishnamurti would allow his teachings to be called a "system"!).

In the present chapter we can break common ground between both schools of thought, because in both the mind is regarded as *the chief culprit* where real esoteric development and self-knowledge are concerned. When we have said earlier that people live entirely in their personalities and believe those personalities to be *themselves,* to all intents and purposes we have referred to their minds. The mind is the chief factor through which the personality functions. There is the physical body, too, but that which gives significance to the personality as a whole is essentially the mind. The mind which controls the working of the personality is therefore the object needing most careful attention if we wish to understand how the personality works.

We have already spoken about the mental body, and about the existence of the higher mental centre and the lower mental centre. In the personality, it is essentially the lower mental centre which operates, and it does this through the intellect, and what is termed *logical thinking*. To the ordinary mind logic is what is assumed to appeal most (although, incidentally, many of its actions are illogical in the extreme).

118

In the mind's approach to everyday things and events it is presumably the logical processes which are brought to bear, although actually the mind works essentially on a pleasure and pain basis. That is to say, apart from those events which do not involve our feelings (where logic and reason can be fully applied), everything which happens to us in our daily lives, every event we meet, is judged or dealt with by one criterion only: *whether it is going to give us pleasure or not.* Not necessarily direct pleasure, but whether the outcome is to be the avoidance of pain in any form, coupled with the desire to achieve pleasure in any form the situation will allow. This is the unfailing attitude of the mind to all its problems, despite all its own beliefs to the contrary. This is because, while *on the surface* paying lip service to reason and logic in the handling of events, under the surface it is our *subconscious* and *unconscious* wishes, desires, fears, inhibitions, etc., which are the real activators of conduct. These have arisen over the years, from infancy upwards, as a result of conditioning factors of various kinds, infantile experiences and urges, etc. which have been repressed or suppressed, and never allowed conscious fulfilment, and which keep up a constant pressure making for irrational action in numerous directions, with the pleasure-pain principle dominant. At the same time, the individual thinks he is living his life quite consciously in accordance with the working of reason and logic. It is really all fantastic and ridiculous, and in a way amusing. Unfortunately, however, the results are so shattering to so many people that it is far from being a laughing matter.

Orthodox psychologists do their best to deal with the upset lives of the people who consult them, but the psychologists are as much the prey to their own lack of knowledge about themselves as are their patients. Their own problems are basically the same as those of the people who consult them, in degree if not in kind, even if the superficial manifestations of their inner malaise are not so self-evident. We do not wish to decry for one moment the very fine work modern psychology is doing in certain directions. The work, however, is very strictly limited. The difference between the "abnormal" people whom the psychiatrist deals with and "normal" folk is very shallow indeed.

In the functioning of the mind, thought is always bound up intimately with feeling or emotion, so that the lower mental centre and the lower emotional centre are always in the very closest relationship. It is emotion which supplies what may be termed propulsive power to thought. As already indicated, the propulsive power of emotion is far too strong for the rational and logical processes under which thought or intellect is usually assumed to function. To have thought without feeling is very rare, indeed; but, on the other hand, we far too often have feeling without very much thought, and that is the usual condition of the general run of people. They consider that they think out their problems, but it is feeling or desire which really rules their conduct. By far the greater portion of the feeling-desire element comes from levels below consciousness, as we have already indicated. If modern psychology has done one thing, it has surely made this fact abundantly clear. Although we personally hold no brief for the theories of many modern psychologists, especially the Psycho-Analytic School, we cannot help but feel that as a body they have done much to make us realize how very lacking in real intelligence are our everyday acts. YET WE CONTINUE THINKING WE ARE INTELLIGENT despite the vast accumulation of evidence to the contrary. This is yet another illustration of the erratic way in which our minds work.

Let us consider again the subject of will, which is usually regarded as merely the result of the pull of the varying desires of the moment. For example, the desire which is the strongest at any one time, under any given conditions, provides the driving force to action. This is regarded as the exercise of will. It is nothing of the sort. Everyday man cannot have true will until he has learned to become more conscious (in the esoteric sense). Real will is an attribute of consciousness, not of the sleep in which most people pass their waking lives. When we consider these matters from the point of view of Esotericism, therefore, we realize how extremely tiny is the amount of real thought we put into the living of our lives. It is a sobering realization indeed. It tends towards the feeling of real humility which is the keynote of those who have begun to understand something real about themselves. The more we know ourselves, the more we realize how petty and trivial and lacking in understanding are our achievements, whether referring to ourselves as individuals (no matter how exalted by worldly standards) or as nations, races, etc. In short, it is only when we realize how little we know that we can set about trying to know (and be) more.

The first essential in this quest is, as we have been trying to show, the realisation that what we think about our minds and mental powers is largely illusory. We have great and wonderful *potentials* for mental development and intellectual achievement, but, so far, in our present sleep state, the level is very low. Yet, despite this fact, we persist in thinking that our mental powers are high. We go around thinking that we can assess everything that happens in the world (and the actual creation and nature and purpose of the Universe itself) by what our minds tell us about such matters. Could we be more presumptuous? In this connection some scientists are by far the worst offenders. They consider that they can use their minds as a sort of yardstick with which to measure the secrets of the Cosmos. The results lead only further into Materialism and Pessimism, because the scientists are following a path which leads only to sterility of thought, and not to enlightenment, despite their wonderful and spectacular but really superficial achievements.

One important thing that Esotericism teaches is that the powers and potentialities of mind are *strictly limited,* no matter how tremendous they may be in themselves. The scope and function of mind has certain limits, because of something inherent in the very fabric of mind. People generally do not realize this (especially scientists, and even psychologists) and much trouble and misery is caused in the world. People continue to feel that they can think their way out of their problems (large or small) and that the mind is the key to everything (despite our very evident inability to use it properly). In fact, as just intimated, mind can go only a certain and very limited part of the way. This is extremely difficult for most people to believe or appreciate, especially philosophers, psychologists, scientists, etc., who set the greatest possible store by thought and logic and the other processes of intellection. That is the chief reason why, today, the blind lead the blind where real guidance in the understanding and living of life is concerned. The wrong guides are appealed to, because they consider that they can solve everything with their minds, which is a sheer impossibility, having regard to the *actual* nature of mind.

For a real understanding of the position we have once again to turn to Esotericism, which makes it abundantly clear that mind was never intended to be as anything other than a servant to man. At present *mind is man's master*. It has been elevated to a position that it was never intended to hold in the cosmic scheme. It has usurped a rôle for which it was never created. The result is that we have lost all possibility of understanding our minds and using them correctly, so that they run away with us as they please. The servant, having got out of control, now leads the master, thanks to the giant cloud of illusion in which we all live. It is only when we begin to appreciate the truth of this that we shall be able to call a halt to the process of the tail wagging the dog. It is a most difficult task, because it means going against the wrong thought of thousands upon thousands of years, with its assumption of leadership of man by his mind and mental apparatus, which has continued unchecked, except in the rare instances in which esoteric training has been undertaken.

An esoteric saying has it that "the mind is the slayer of the real". *Until we appreciate the truth of this statement,* and begin to see its relevance to our day-to-day lives, we shall be unable to find our way out of the morass in living in which we are at present bogged down. In order to understand what is implied by the above saying, we must turn again to what was said in a previous chapter about the various centres, i.e., mental, emotional, instinctive, etc. It was said that there is the higher mental centre and the lower mental centre, and that it is the lower mental centre which is the seat of the ordinary mind or intellect. This mind functions through the brain and nervous system, and is closely bound up with the senses, which bring to the brain (via the nervous system) certain stimuli which convey to the mind (via the brain) news of what is happening in the world outside ourselves, and also in the world inside ourselves.

The mind or intellect functions essentially through the physical basis of brain, nervous system and sense organs, and is quite incapable of functioning without them. Therefore the mind is tied by them, and cannot cope with anything or understand anything which does not come to it via these media. This means to say that if we believe (as by far the vast majority of people do) that through our minds we are capable of assessing "Reality" or "the Universe" or "God", and be able to make authoritative pronouncements about such basic concepts, we are living in a fool's paradise.

We must realize that the minds with which we endeavour to assess such mighty conceptions are themselves only capable of functioning at a level at which these basic realities cannot possibly be understood, except as intellectual theories which the mind has already reduced to its own dimensions. In other words, before the mind can grapple with any problem it has to bring it down to a level where the senses can operate on it and transmit impressions about it to the brain via the nervous system. Any problem which is greater than man or the mind he possesses must inevitably be beyond mental approach by man, unless man considers that everything in the Universe is of a similar or lower stature or status than himself. Man does not see the issue in this light, especially scientists. That, however, is precisely what the situation amounts to once we realize the limitations under which the mind of man operates.

With the technical apparatus now available man can reach out to the farthest stars and examine them, and delve into the very core of matter, but he is still immersed in his senses and what his senses bring to him via the instruments he uses. Therefore, he is still bound by, and the prisoner of, his senses and brain and nervous system in his assessment of these vast and fundamental problems. When, for instance, a scientist thinks he is measuring a star billions of miles away, he is actually making a computation which is a combination of the reality which is there and what his senses tell him about it. He does not contact the reality itself, only something which his senses construct for him from the data surrounding that reality as capable of being experienced by his senses. Anything beyond the scope of his senses is incapable of being assessed, so that the world which science has revealed to us, and any computations or theories derived therefrom, are purely relative, i.e., relative to man's own mental apparatus and the brain, nervous system and sense organs which he possesses.

We can say, therefore, that "the mind is the slayer of the real", because in the attempt to approach reality, in whatever form, that reality is immediately shattered by the very fact that the mind has attempted to make judgments or theories about it. Thus, the more the mind seeks to pry into reality the farther does reality retreat from it. This will still apply regardless of how much more wonderful the paraphernalia of science continues to become. Let man invent telescopes of the greatest magnitude, or microscopes of no matter what power, he still will not be able to understand what matter really is, or what a star is, let alone the even more fundamental factors of creation which lie at the back of them.

Once we acknowledge and realize the limitations of mind, it brings to us a kind of peace. We cease trying vainly to understand the secrets of the Universe as we have hitherto tried to do. We come to the point where we realize that another way of approach has to be tried, to get in touch with, and try to understand, these basic and fundamental realities of life and existence. *And that is precisely where the higher mental centre comes in.* It is this centre which has the ability and power to contact the basic realities of the Cosmos, and it works quite differently from the ordinary mind or intellect, which is domiciled in the lower mental centre, and which functions through the more external part of that centre. The higher mental centre functions through intuition and illumination, but also it is connected with the inner part of the lower mental centre, and thus has contact with man's psycho-physical organism. Its knowledge comes to it *direct.* Not through the medium of the brain and nervous system and the ordinary sense organs. It functions at a much higher level than that, and can consequently contact and gain knowledge of things which are quite beyond the reach of the ordinary mind.

All the real understanding of the Universe accumulated by Esotericism throughout the ages has come to man via the higher mental centre. That is why those with real esoteric training and development are in touch with a level of life and understanding quite impossible of achievement by ordinary man, via his day-to-day mind. With the higher mental centre is associated the functioning of the higher emotional centre, just as with the lower mental centre there is always associated the working of the lower emotional centre. With the real inner illumination which comes from the higher mental centre comes also that deep love and wonder

and mystery which enwraps man when he is able to gain some
contact with the everlasting realities of our wonderful Cosmos.
The ecstasies of the true mystic and seer come from this
source, simply because he has arrived at a point in his inner
development where the working of both his higher mental and
higher emotional centres have begun to be felt directly by
him.

Strange as it may sound, the higher mental and higher
emotional centres are always fully operative in all of us,
even as we are at present. It is only by work on ourselves, and
real esoteric inner development, that we can become capable
of contacting the higher centres within us, which at present
we cannot contact because of the continual clamour set up
by the personality. This, indeed, is the central truth which
esoteric training seeks constantly to inculcate into the candidate for esoteric development. He does not have to try to
develop his higher centres. He has them already, fully
developed, anxious for us to contact them. As we now are, we
have no link within us which can make this contact possible.
It is only the development of essence within us which can
supply that link; and essence can only grow, as we have
already indicated, through the progressive damping-down of
the personality with its egocentricity and self-love. Only by
making personality passive can essence become active, and
provide the link between us and our higher centres. This
knowledge is of priceless value to us when we understand
what it truly implies.

Before concluding this chapter on the limitations of mind,
and the processes of logical thinking, it will be as well to say
something about ideas. Ideas are the food of thought, as it
were. In the vast majority of cases ideas are used as if they
were real things in themselves, instead of being only mental
agglomerations of words or thoughts. Words and thoughts
are necessary for ideas to be developed, and our minds feed
on such ideas, as just said. The great trouble with the vast

majority of us, however, is that we think that ideas are real *in themselves*, instead of just being signposts pointing towards something more fundamental and real.

For instance, many people think that ideas about "God" or "Reality" or "Consciousness" are the very things themselves; just as many people think that ideas about "Socialism" or "Communism" or "Conservatism" are real things with validity in themselves. They live their lives amidst such ideas (mental furniture) and consider that by having the ideas they really are Socialists or Communists or Conservatives. In exactly the same way many religious-minded people believe they are aware of "God" merely because of certain ideas about "Him" which they have in their mind. The world is full of such ideas, and unless translated into reality they are pernicious because they render all our thoughts and mental activity sterile.

All that we are writing about are ideas, but ideas which can transform us into entirely different people, *if acted upon*. If they remain merely ideas, they are useless. It is up to us to sift the worth-while ideas from the worthless ones, and then *translate them into action* in our lives, in whatever realm they may apply.

Continuing, let us try to show the reader the real place of the mind or intellect in the daily scheme of things. It would be quite wrong to let people assume, from what we have been saying, that the ordinary mind or intellect has no use or value at all. Of course it has, and a very great value, indeed. BUT IN ITS RIGHTFUL SPHERE AND PLACE. It is when the mind tries to usurp the leadership of the individual that it gets out of its proper sphere and into one where it does not rightfully belong. When we live in the personality it is only natural for the mind to lead, because, as we have already shown, the personality functions exclusively through the mind, aided by the physical body and emotions, via the instinctive-moving, and lower emotional centres.

Once we begin to realize, however, that the personality is not our real self, merely an imposter masquerading as ourself, then mind has to be put severely into its place. Instead of being the master of man it has to become his servant, eager and willing to carry out all his behests. Once such a position has been reached, mind has taken up its rightful place in the cosmic scheme of things, allowing the higher mental centre to do all the directing and the ordinary intellect or mind to do all the carrying out of the commands thus issued to it. When we have such a condition in any individual man or woman, we may say that here mind is serving its proper function as the hand-maid of man. In this capacity it can be of the greatest possible service to him. In the realm of computing, working out intricate details, the development of associations of ideas, imagery, memory, etc., the ordinary everyday mind is invaluable to man. It is only when it tries to make him believe that it can tell him all about the secrets of the Universe, and about his own origin and destiny, etc., that it shows its falseness. As already made clear, all the more fundamental capacities are the sole responsibility of the higher mental centre, which works in us through intuition and inner illumination, linked up in us with the working of the higher emotional centre.

Therefore, for the higher mental centre to begin to function properly, the *ordinary mind* must first realize that it is incapable of carrying out the tasks which only the *higher mental centre* can fulfil. When it does realize this fact it stops struggling and fighting to do what it was never intended to do, and becomes still and silent. It is only when the ordinary mind gets into this passive state, instead of its present state of ceaseless activity, that the ideas and promptings from the higher mental centre can percolate down to us *via the inner part of the lower mental centre.*

At present, in its over-active and highly inflammable and excitable condition, the mind or intellect is the great stumbling-block which prevents the ideas and promptings from the higher mental centre coming down to us. Once, however, it has realized the truth of what we have been saying in the present chapter, and accepts the fact of its own limitation, it becomes still of its own volition. It can then begin to be the mirror for the higher mental centre (or higher mind) which it was originally intended to be. When this *rapport* between the higher and lower mind has been achieved, the ordinary mind or intellect has assumed its rightful place in man's internal economy. There will no longer be the eternal conflict between thought and reality which at present besets us all. We shall be able to interpret reality through our minds, via the higher mental centre, and be able to live in direct relation with it. *That is exactly what Esotericism sets out to teach us to do.*

In this present chapter we have set out to give the reader some idea of the way in which the mind and the processes of rational thinking are regarded in the Gurdjieff system of esoteric development. Students of Krishnamurti will easily see how what we have been saying ties up very closely with what he himself has to say on this most fundamental issue, albeit perhaps not in the same words. The underlying principle is the same in both teachings, we feel, even if the words and ideas used are not identical. This must necessarily be so because both teachers seek to direct men's minds into channels wherein man can begin to become *himself* and not the caricature of himself which he now is. To achieve this all-important objective it is essential to understand clearly the limitations of the mind or intellect, and its legitimate uses as apart from its all too prevalent abuses in the world of today.

Special note. A very important difference between the lower and higher mental centres, is that to the lower mind everything is fragmentary and separate, i.e., it separates things and breaks them down. Whereas to the higher mind there is always *unity* underlying all diversity. In other words the higher mind unites, and the lower one divides. Most of the functioning of the lower mental centre is done through the external part, called the formatory part. The middle and inner parts of this centre are capable of linking up with the higher mental centre under appropriate conditions, such as we have referred to earlier in the present chapter.

CHAPTER XVII

THREE UNIVERSAL FORCES

IN this chapter we wish to deal with a teaching of The Work
that has great importance, not only on the theoretical side, but
for its everyday practical use. We refer to the teaching about
THREE FORCES. In all ancient Cosmogonies there is always
reference to the building of the Universe by means of triads
of forces, each successive stage of creation being carried out
by its own particular triad. In the Christian teaching about
The Trinity we have this same viewpoint expressed. For anything of real cosmic significance there are always *three factors
involved*. This is most easily seen in the three related gods of
the Hindu religion: Brahmâ, Vishnu, and Shiva. Brahmâ is
the creator; Vishnu *the preserver;* and Shiva *the destroyer*.
Wherever there is creation there must also be destruction to
create a balance, otherwise creation would over-populate the
world and thereby thwart its own intention. Therefore, there
must be the contrary power of destruction to keep a sort of
check on creation, and there must also be the third power of
preservation at work, too, to stabilize the operation of the
whole scheme. In this simple illustration we have the model
of all other triads or triadic forces at work in the Universe,
and The Work teaching we wish to discuss in the present
chapter falls into this category. *First force* is active, *second
force* is negative or opposing force, and *third force* is neutra-
lising or balancing force.

In the everyday world we know of only two kinds of forces,
as for instance the scientific ideas of positive and negative;

attraction and repulsion; active and passive; plus and minus, etc. The idea of the existence of a third force, which balances the other two opposing forces, has received no recognition in any way. The world is all the poorer as a result, because it has lost a key of tremendous significance, which could do much to make clear many problems which at present bewilder and bedevil the lives of most of us. If we believe that there are only two forces at work in any problem or situation, we turn all our attention to these two factors and seek to find a solution which will sort out the difficulties between them. As we do not know of the existence of the *third force* it stands to reason that our solution of the problem, whatever it may be, is bound to be faulty. That is why The Work teaching about the three forces is such an important key to the unravelling of some of our greatest difficulties. Let us give one or two simple examples of what we mean :

Supposing one wishes to climb a mountain, the desire to climb the mountain is first force, in this instance. But the desire to climb the mountain inevitably calls into existence second force, which always arises in direct opposition to first force, no matter what first force may be in any particular situation. In this instance second force is the mountain itself, with all its difficulties in the way of height, slippery rocks, weather conditions, etc. Thus a third force is required to enable the desire to climb the mountain (first force) to overcome the opposition of the mountain itself (second force), and the third force is the skill and determination of the climber. If his skill and determination are sufficient for his task, he will achieve his objective; if they are not sufficient, he will not.

That is a very simple illustration of what we mean by three forces always being operative in any given situation or problem, but the ramifications go much deeper than appear on the surface. For instance, not many people realize that as soon as they set up an objective for themselves, no matter what, opposition to it must arise inevitably, in one form or another, in accordance with the law of the three forces. We do not always see what the second force may be, in any given situation or circumstance. It is always there, however, because the very fact of our setting out to achieve any particular objective (first force) must set in motion second force to oppose it. When we look back over our lives we can see countless illustrations of this fact. If we had known then of the existence of this cosmic law, how different things might have been!

For instance, let us suppose we wanted to train for a certain career, and that we set out to try to carry out our desire in that direction. Much to our surprise, and possibly dismay, however, we found all sorts of obstacles to our path which made it exceedingly difficult for us to carry out our initial desire. We did not realize why we met obstacles because we did not know anything about the teaching of the three forces. If we had been aware of it we would have been prepared for the obstacles, *because we would have known that their presence was inevitable.* Every effort in life brings its contrary effort to oppose it, because it is the way of life. It will therefore depend upon what type of *third force* we employ, in any given situation, as to whether we shall be able to overcome the second force or be overcome by it.

Once we see matters in this light, many things which were not understood are now made clear. The more blindly we act in any given situation, the more likely is second force to gain the day; because ignorance adds greatly to the power of second force, as knowledge adds greatly to the power of the third force which we may bring to bear. Hence the great value of this teaching in ordinary life. It has a far deeper value, however, on the esoteric side.

In all ordinary affairs, third force is provided by life, i.e., by the events of life as dictated by ambition, lust, greed, pride, vanity, etc. The result is that we are glued more firmly than ever to life and its grip on the personality side of ourselves.

Therefore, if we wish to work on ourself, and free ourself from the grip of life on our personality, in any given situation, we must transform the third force, previously provided by life, into a third force provided by The Work. If we do this, the whole situation becomes entirely transformed. The result of the interaction of the three forces in any ordinary situation is now quite different. This is because when we use The Work as third force the polarity of our aim is reversed from what it was previously, when life was paramount. Our aim is different, because we are now trying to make personality passive, whereas before personality was active. Therefore, in reversing our aim we reverse the effect of any given situation, because a different third force is brought to bear on it. That is why *aim* is so much talked about in The Work teachings, because it depends upon our aim as to what the third force shall be in dealing with our day-to-day problems and difficulties.

To make this point quite clear let us suppose that one had wanted to be a great singer. Then the desire to become a singer would be first force. This would inevitably bring up second force in the shape of all sorts of obstacles to this project : parental opposition, perhaps, lack of funds for training purposes, having to work at a job which interfered with tuition, etc. But the third force which would tend to overcome second force in the *life* sense would be *ambition* (plus talent, of course). If the ambition was strong enough, and the talent was there, second force could probably be overcome in time, and so in due course the desire to become a great singer would be realized.

If, however, the individual had acted from the ideas of The Work, ambition (which is connected with the false personality) would not be operative, so that a different kind of third force would be required, one that did not have any relation to false personality and which did not seek to boost it in any way and accentuate its pride and vanity, etc. Thus, if the individual felt really deeply that singing was his real vocation, he would use as third force the desire to give real expression to something real and vital within himself, which he feels he must try to express at all cost, no matter what hardships or privations he may have to endure.

This is entirely different from the driving power of ambition, which seeks fame, wealth, and the adulation of the world; it is something much more real and valid and valuable (in the inner esoteric sense). Thus the individual would be working for an entirely different aim and for something which was of real inner value to him, not something which merely fed his false personality, as when ambition supplied the motive power of third force. Also, in this instance where third force was supplied by The Work, and not ambition, the person concerned would know at once whether he really had the gift of song within him, or if he had not. If it was an inferior talent he was trying to foster, he would stop training to be a singer and give up the project altogether. He would know it was the result of something false within him. If, however, the third force was provided by ambition, he would not have this criterion to guide him.

This whole teaching is of tremendous significance, and shows what the effect of The Work training can be on our lives in all departments of living. Summarized, it means that the difference of aim would immediately transform the third force in any given situation, bringing about directly contrary results, according to whether third force came from life or from The Work.

As we can touch only lightly upon this vitally important teaching in this book, for many illuminating illustrations of the subject we must refer the reader to Dr. Nicoll's *Psychological Commentaries*. Incidentally, this is a topic on which Krishnamurti does not touch in his teachings, as far as our knowledge goes.

CHAPTER XVIII

GAINING AND LOSING FORCE

THE interesting point about the esoteric system we are discussing is that it not only helps to transform us into entirely different beings, beings far finer and greater in every way than we have been hitherto, but it also helps to make our day-to-day lives far more interesting and *practical,* too. That is to say, we do not remove ourselves from the practical affairs of daily living and live in a world remote and removed from the stresses and strains of ordinary existence; we still live in that world, *but far more consciously and effectively because of our work upon ourselves.* A case in point is The Work teaching about *gaining and losing force.*

In the ordinary way we squander the force (or vitality) which we possess in all sorts of detrimental ways in carrying out the pursuits of the personality. It is a teaching of The Work that we have only a certain quantity of force or vitality at our disposal each day, so that it stands to reason that if the amount of force is frittered away needlessly or purposelessly, we shall be the poorer to that extent and not be able to do anything worthwhile or constructive that day. If this squandering of force goes on day after day, as it does with the great majority of people, then we can all realize that nothing of real worth can be accomplished in our lives. We shall be just useless members of society, no matter how high and exalted our position may be in that society.

Many of the things that fascinate and draw the personality into action in its daily affairs, tend to make us lose force, albeit at the time we may feel we are gaining something of value to ourselves. But the gain is merely illusory, as are so many of the supposed gains of the personality, which keep us all the more chained to it and completely identified with it. One of the chief ways in which we lose force is through what—in The Work— is called Inner Talking* which goes on in us most of the day. Another equally potent source of loss of force is self-justifying, while all negative emotions drain force from us. Therefore, as most people are engaged in these activities most of the day, it will be easy to see from this how much force is lost each day. *People are forever losing force!*

How can we *gain* force? This is something which The Work definitely teaches, through such techniques as Self-Remembering, Self-Observation, Non-Identification, etc. Indeed, in one aspect, the whole purpose of The Work is to make us gain force, in order that we may be the more able to carry out the work of self-transformation which is its chief objective. To achieve that objective we need a lot of force, far more than that usually available to the average individual of today. Emphasis is also laid, in The Work teachings, upon being able to relax physically as much as possible, as physical relaxation is another important aid to conserving force (if not to actually gaining any). It stands to reason that, the more we can relax our bodies and keep free from bodily tensions, strains, etc., the more scope will there be for the use of our inherent vitality or force.

In regard to the question of gaining and losing force, we may usefully turn for a moment to The Work teaching about *The Pendulum.* In our ordinary state we are usually either excited or depressed; either very pleased with ourselves, or very cast down about our affairs in general. That is to say,

---

* This subject has been dealt with more fully in a previous chapter.

we do not continue on an even keel, but are always either at one end of the pendulum's swing or at the other, the pendulum denoting the two extremes of emotional instability, the two extremes within which we swing continually throughout the day. We never achieve a position midway between the swings for very long. Our immersion in daily life tends to make us extremely vulnerable to the swing of the pendulum from one extreme to the other, under the driving power of the personality. We can all test this for ourselves if we can view our daily lives without identification for a moment.

In The Work we are exhorted to try to note the constant swing of the pendulum which carries us from excitement to depression, from elation to gloom, etc., with each event that happens to us; so that, in time, we may achieve a balanced position midway between the swings. By doing this we will not only be doing very much to increase our conscious control of ourselves and our awareness generally, but we shall also be gaining a great deal of force. As already indicated, it is essential to gain that force if we are to carry through the transformation of ourselves which is the aim of The Work. Thus it will be seen how all aspects of The Work impinge on one another and reinforce and underline each other in all kinds of ways. There is mutual interdependence all round.

One of the chief ways of losing force—apart from those already mentioned—is "being between centres". This term means that the individual is not in direct connection with any of his centres, which we have already spoken about. The reader will remember that there are various centres in the human entity, the instinctive-moving centre on the physiological level; the emotional centre on the emotional level; and the mental centre on the mental level. (We are leaving out the higher centres, as they do not come into play in our ordinary everyday lives.) When we are "in attention" in any one of the centres referred to, and using it purposefully, then we are utilizing our force wisely and beneficially, and may even gain force. That would be, for instance, when doing some manual work in the control of the instinctive-moving centre, or playing a game, such as tennis, or swimming, or taking a vigorous walk, etc.; or when feeling something with intensity, in the full control of the emotional centre, as when listening to a gripping play, etc.; or when reading or working with intensity and properly-directed effort, under the control of the mental centre, etc.

All effort in full relationship with a centre either uses force wisely, or can even gain force for us, depending upon its nature and direction; more than one centre can be actively co-operating with one or the other centres, at the same time, in some special type of activity; or all three can be in play together, as in some forms of dramatic art, dancing, and the like. In such cases force is definitely gained by such a combined use of centres; and, indeed, Gurdjieff himself set great store by properly-directed dance movements, which brought all centres into operation together, and could, in fact, under his direction, bring the student into contact with higher centres, too.

But "being between centres" means not being in direct relationship with any centre at all, and is the complete antithesis of properly-directed work of any kind. It is then that we lose force in a big way, as it were, and it applies to all those occasions—so frequent in everyday life—when we do not know what to do with ourselves; when we cannot make up our mind whether to do this or to do that; or when we feel bored and unable to do anything but just sit around feeling "fed up" with ourselves and with life in general; and so forth. These are the occasions when we are "between centres", and force is drained from us as a consequence, and we can prove it (once we are aware of the fact) by the way in which we feel at such times. We do, indeed, feel drained of all energy and are listless and without any motive force whatever. The only way in which we can counter such a situation, once we are aware of what is occurring, is to get into a centre right away and do something positive, whether of a physical, emotional or mental nature (or a combination of them). Then we stop the drain of force brought about by being between centres, and may even gain some force instead, depending entirely upon what we are doing, or thinking, etc.

Thus the teaching about gaining and losing force has direct practical relationship to our daily lives, besides making us aware of something most important to our esoteric develop- ment generally. We could deal with the subject from other angles, showing how force can be gained or lost in a variety of different ways; but for the purposes of the present book we feel we have given the reader sufficient indication of the rudi- ments of another important teaching of The Work.

Before concluding this chapter, however, it should be made clear that, when thinking or talking about force or energy, The Work posits *four entirely different types of force or energy,* none of which can be changed or resolved into any of the others. In the ordinary way people regard energy as one thing, no matter in what field it may be exerted or encoun- tered, and modern science is equally guilty of holding the same belief, which has crept into most views about the sub- ject, giving it a decidedly materialistic tinge. But The Work lays it down categorically that four different types of energy exist on different levels, and the energy on one level is entirely different from the energy on another level. This, therefore, gives us a completely different viewpoint on this very impor- tant subject, and a viewpoint which has many important repercussions, not the least in the psychological and philo- sophical fields.

The four types of force or energy are :

(1) *Ordinary mechanical energy* derived from steam, heat, electricity, the atom, etc., and utilised for the working of machines and everything man-made.

(2) *Vital energy* which is the energy of the body and of all living things.

(3) *Psychic energy* or the energy which makes us think and feel, i.e., mental and emotional energy.

(4) *Conscious energy*, the energy of spirit or consciousness.

The Work lays it down that these four categories of force or energy are quite distinct each from the other, and that mechanical energy can never become vital energy; that vital energy can never become psychic energy; and that psychic energy can never become conscious energy. Once we realize the truth of these statements, it makes us see the whole matter in an entirely new light.

The Work once again reveals a fundamental working of the Cosmos which ordinarily is unknown to both scientist and layman alike. It provides a key which can help us to unlock hidden doors to further esoteric understanding. In a sense we may say that the transformation of grosser energies into finer ones, is the whole secret of The Work. It is real Alchemy.

CHAPTER XIX

TIME AND ETERNITY

WE wish to say something, now, about time and eternity, immortality, rebirth, etc., all subjects of fundamental importance to the student of Esotericism. In his book, *Living Time,* Dr. Nicoll has elaborated a viewpoint about time to which Ouspensky had made some reference in *A New Model of the Universe,* in which time is regarded as something which is not just a matter of duration, but as something having reality in itself. By this we mean that, to the ordinary mind, time is regarded as merely duration, i.e., some medium through and in which things or events happen or take place, but which itself is always passing away. We break up time into past, present and future. The present is always the single point which divides the past from the future, and it is always slipping into the past as we look at it. According to the conception referred to above, time is held to be something far more fundamental than this; it is held to be a *dimension* IN WHICH EVENTS ARE ALWAYS TAKING PLACE AND HAVING ONCE TAKEN PLACE ARE ALWAYS *THERE,* even if time itself seems to have passed on. *The past is not something which has vanished into thin air,* as it were, as is usually assumed. The past still exists in its own dimension (in the time dimension) and can be recalled and re-lived under the appropriate stimuli or conditions. It is also accepted that the future is already in existence (even though we have not yet contacted it), just as the past exists (even though we think it is finished and done with).

This very different conception of time may seem most

strange at first sight. It is essentially the esoteric viewpoint, indicating how the whole life of man is linked up from birth to death, into one unity, and that no part of the life can be separated from what has gone before or is going to come after. Thus the life of man is given a coherence and unity with which the ordinary view of time does not supply him. He feels that the past is dead and gone and the future has not yet arrived; yet the present in which he lives is so narrow a reality that he feels, in a sense, that it is the past which is far more real. The past, although no longer existent, seems to him much more real and solid than the ever-changing present, or the not-yet-reached future. If, however, we once accept the idea of ourselves as living in a time which contains within it —in living form—all that has already happened to us and will happen to us in the future, we immediately obtain an entirely different view of ourselves and of our relationship to the Cosmos generally. We become much more *real people*.

As part of the common view that time is something which is always passing, there is also the belief that eternity is something which exists somewhere a long way off and that it is of endless duration. From the esoteric standpoint, eternity is viewed as being something which exists *here and now*, and is always in contact with ordinary time, interpenetrating it at every point (if we can but contact it). That is to say, eternity is not something distant from us—something outside of ordinary time—it is simply another level which exists coincidentally with ordinary time. This level we can enter when we leave our ordinary personality-driven life and go into the realm of the more real part of ourselves, i.e., REAL "I". In short, REAL "I" *lives in eternity*. That is its habitat, and when we enter that part of ourselves we are at once in eternity.

This sounds very strange to people whose thought runs along conventional lines. That is because they have never properly understood the real meaning and nature of eternity. Eternity is something which is here and now, but which those of us who live in the personality never contact. We live in ordinary time and know nothing about this other dimension of living. To people who live in their real selves (REAL "I") eternity is their ordinary realm of living, just as ordinary time is our realm of living. Once we understand the truth of this statement, everything becomes quite different. It explains why such great beings as Christ, Buddha, Krishna, etc., talk about themselves in the way they do. They live in eternity, but also in the same time as we do; only to them it is the eternal which is the reality, while our time is the illusion. Whereas to us it is our time which is the reality and eternity the illusion. Occasionally we can break through into eternity, even in our everyday lives, if we contact the more real part of ourselves through some unusual experience, and then for a moment we partake of eternity, *which is the home of reality*. We feel afterwards that we have had an experience which is so profound that we shall remember it to our dying day. This is purely because when we do contact the eternal we are actually living in the highest part of ourselves for that instant, and have stepped out of ordinary time into eternity.

The greater the individual (i.e., the more he lives in the real part of himself and not in the personality) the more time will he spend in eternity, even though living a seemingly ordinary life here on earth. *This is a most important fact to grasp,* therefore, for all really creative work of any kind, and all real mystic experiences, all genuine seership, etc., take place or are lived in the realm of eternity, although seemingly taking place in our own time and space. The two realms are so intertwined in actuality, that one can live in both without other people being in the least aware of the fact. Only we can be aware of it, by the effect it has upon us; because one moment of life in eternity is incomparable with a whole life-time lived in ordinary time. One can therefore put forward the following axiom : the more a man or woman lives in the real centre of themselves, the more will they contact the eternal and live in eternity, even though they are living their day-to-day lives in ordinary time. Eternity in the real sense has nothing whatever to do with life after death, or life beyond the grave; it is capable of being experienced and lived in *right now,* this very instant, should conditions be such that we are capable of rising sufficiently out of our everyday personalities to allow this to occur. Thus eternity has nothing to do with immortality, although in another sense these two are very closely related.

The point is that, the more we can live in the more essential part of ourselves, the more opportunity will there be for *REAL I* to operate through us, and the more, therefore, will we be living in eternity. Also, the more of us that will remain after the death of the physical body. This is indeed a very profound issue to understand. Here is a little illumination on the subject : in Christianity and other types of orthodox religion it is assumed that when the body dies the soul or spirit remains and lives on in eternity (a time of endless duration, being similar to our own time but never-ending). But people who live their lives solely in their personalities (as the vast majority of us do) have nothing developed inside them really capable of surviving as immortal after death.

Immortality is something which has to be earned (in Gurdjieff's phrase); and the only way we can earn it is by *working on ourselves.* The more we work on ourselves esoterically the greater shall we develop the more internal parts of ourselves (i.e., the second and third bodies). It is only these deeper internal bodies which can survive after the death of the physical body, and so confer on us immortality. The more the interior bodies have been developed during life, the more there will remain after death, and the more unified will be the inner reality of the individual concerned. That is the only type of immortality which is of value.

It is not meant to infer that when we ordinary people die that is the end of us. Far from it. When the physical body dies there still remains the very interior parts of us to continue life in another realm or dimension. So long as our more subtle bodies are not properly developed, the time spent in the after-death state will be one of comparative unconsciousness. There will be no conscious experience of the after-death spheres. Thus, immortality indicates the ability to live *consciously* in the after-death spheres (in the higher realms of the Cosmos), and has nothing to do with living in eternity. Although it must be realized that people who achieve immortality do live in eternity, to a considerable degree, during their earth-life, because in that earth-life they have lived in the higher parts of themselves; those parts which confer immortality on us after death. This may seem very involved, but we hope the reader will be able to gain some glimpse of what is meant.

The whole point is that space and time are essential ingredients of the mental furniture of the *ordinary* mind. It cannot think without these concepts, and everything it does think about *must* take place within space and time. Therefore, the ordinary mind cannot conceive of anything happening which does not happen within space and time. When we transcend the ordinary mind, as when we function in the higher mental centre, thinking in that realm can take place quite outside the confines of space and time, and events can be appreciated in an entirely different context. Time is then seen as being something quite different from a mere movement of events in one continuous direction from the past to present and future. Time is appreciated as something *in itself*, something which has a reality of its own; and the past, the present, and the future are seen as *altogether*, existing as one. It is the everyday rational mind which breaks down time into past, present and future. In the higher mental realms, the future is just as much in existence now as the past; so that pre-vision and pre-cognition are quite understandable phenomena when we realize that it is only the lower or ordinary mind which is incapable of contacting such strata of comprehension. When we have to think about such subjects as immortality and "life after death", we must always bear in mind that such concepts are meaningless to our ordinary level of thinking. They have significance or meaning only when we transcend the normal space-time working of our thought processes.

This brings us to the subject of Rebirth, which is not strictly part of the Gurdjieff system, but which we feel is something worth discussing at the present juncture in order to make certain of the foregoing points more clear. To those who are familiar with the age-old teachings about *Reincarnation* and *Karma,* which are fundamental to all Eastern religions, what we have been saying in the present chapter will be quite readily understood.

Once those teachings are understood there will be a most profound difference in the way in which we look at life and at ourselves. We begin to see that this life we are living is only one of a series of lives which we are living on earth, during which process we are learning certain lessons which the higher part of ourselves knows it is essential for us to learn. If we do not learn them in one life, then we have to learn them in the next, or the one after that, and so forth. Thus we keep on returning to earth (in a different physical vehicle and personality each time, but linked with those previously shed through Karma), and this cycle of rebirth continues on until (possibly aeons hence) we have learnt all that earth-life can teach us and further rebirth is then no longer necessary.

The teaching about Karma is that what we sow in one life we have to reap in that life or succeeding lives, so that everything that happens to us is always the result of *our own actions,* and not just the working of some malign influence, or the outcome of chance or accident. After death there is a period during which the higher bodies work out their own destiny in the after-death spheres, until the time comes for a fresh earth life, when the cycle of reincarnation proceeds.

When we realize that our destiny—not only in this present life, but in those yet to come—depends entirely upon what we make of our lives here and now, an entirely new light is thrown upon our position in the scheme of things. Instead of just allowing ourselves to drift along on the tide of events, as heretofore, we begin to see the need to do something about the matter; *we begin to feel that we ourselves are responsible for our future,* not only in this life but in lives yet unlived. All this underlines the vital need to begin to work on ourselves, along the lines of "The Work", because only so can we begin to bring about any changes both in ourselves and our circumstances, not only for the remainder of this life, but for future lives. Otherwise we shall just continue going round in a sort of squirrel-cage, life after life, each life being more or less an exact replica of the life previously lived.

We are dealing with weighty subjects, indeed. Because Western people have never thought about rebirth, and the whole subject seems quite strange and possibly ridiculous to them, it does not mean that we have to dismiss it as being so. There are many things the Western mind has to learn and which the East is waiting to teach it. Rebirth is one of those subjects. An increasing number of the most brilliant Western thinkers are turning to the East for enlightenment—people such as Aldous Huxley, Gerald Heard, etc., and that is an indication that the West is beginning to appreciate what the East has to teach. By bringing Theosophy to the Western World at the latter part of the last century, Madame H. P. Blavatsky did more than any other single individual to make the wisdom of the ancient East available to the more receptive of Western thinkers.

The esoteric view about time, eternity, immortality, rebirth, etc., gives us much food for thought, therefore. The more we ponder about these basic concepts the more do we realize what a lot Western people have to learn about such things.

They are foreign to our everyday mode of thinking. We are limited by that mode of thinking in trying to understand what such conceptions really mean and what they imply. We have to "break the moulds of mind" in order to do so. We have to divest ourselves of the shackles in which our minds have been imprisoned all our lives, in order to be able to appreciate Esotericism.

In this connection it is important to bear in mind that immortality has nothing to do with rebirth. Rebirth may be termed an automatic cosmic process. We all go on being re-born for life after life, as already indicated, and this has nothing to do with being immortal. Immortality has relevance only to something within us which is *indestructible;* something within us which can survive death, time after time, as each rebirth takes place. It is that part of ourselves which is distinct from personality, *the more real and fundamental part of ourselves,* which is immortal. The more we can work on ourselves through any one life, and make the fundamental part of ourselves known to us and live in it, the more immortality shall we gain for ourselves. Because that is the part of ourselves which is outside of ordinary rebirth in the sense that it is *always enduring through time.*

It is interesting to note that Gurdjieff did not have anything to say in his teachings about rebirth, although he stressed the need for working on ourselves in order to secure immortality. His idea evidently was that if people thought they had other lives they would not put as much effort into work on them-selves in the present life. Therefore, he said nothing about future lives. His emphasis was all on *this* life and the immediate present. And exactly the same is true about Krishnamurti. He, too, says nothing about future lives, and stresses only the present life. Being a Hindu he would naturally accept *Reincarnation* and *Karma.* When questioned on these points he reiterated that it is only the personality which is so intent on trying to live again, to continue even

after death. He emphasizes that it is this part of ourselves
which is the great illusion and keeps us from knowing Reality,
God, Truth, etc. Therefore, he said nothing about such subjects as rebirth, etc., feeling, no doubt, that—as Gurdjieff does
—they distract us from the immediate task in hand, which is
to effect our emancipation from the thralldom of the personality, the deadly enemy which keeps us all firmly within
its grip.

The next chapter is devoted to a brief summary of the
teachings of Krishnamurti, as we feel that basically they are
in line with the esoteric system with which the present book is
mainly concerned. As just said, and no doubt for the reason
just given, he has nothing to say about the question of rebirth.

CHAPTER XX

A CHAPTER ON KRISHNAMURTI

WE have decided to say something about the writings of
Krishnamurti because fundamentally they are similar to those
put forward in the Gurdjieff system, although expressed in
somewhat different terms. At first reading many people may
be inclined to say that there is no resemblance between the
two expositions; but when one has really become acquainted
with them, and studied them both carefully, it is obvious that
they are talking about the same things, i.e., *man's need for real
knowledge of himself as the initial step towards real understanding and ability to live properly in a world that does not
know what such real living means.*

The writer has been interested in Krishnamurti—on and off
—for over thirty years, but he could not grasp his essential
meaning until recently. He sensed that there was something
"real", but he always felt that it was "truth in a vacuum",
meaning by this that he did not see how Krishnamurti's views
could be applied to present-day life by ordinary men and
women. In short, he could not obtain the central clue to what
Krishnamurti was talking about. It was only after beginning
to study Dr. Nicoll's *Commentaries* that he saw more clearly
what it was that Krishnamurti meant. At just about this time,
too, he became acquainted with someone who, he felt—at last
—really did understand Krishnamurti and who was the
practical embodiment of those views in his personal life.

151

There are many people who claim that they understand Krishnamurti and seek to interpret him to all and sundry. To the present writer's mind, however, such people are more often than not right off the real track and following some path of their own which they say is Krishnamurti's. It is so deadly easy to delude oneself in these matters, all the more so because—in the present instance—what Krishnamurti has to say is quite unintelligible to the ordinary rational mind. With the limitations that the rational mind has, it is quite impossible to follow Krishnamurti's trend of thought, which means that it is all too easy to interpret him in any way one chooses. Therefore, there are many false prophets telling people that *they* understand Krishnamurti and know exactly about what he is talking.

But, as just said, it was the writer's good fortune to become acquainted with a student of Krishnamurti some time ago, who, we feel, *really does understand him.* It is because of what we have learned from this one individual that we feel that we can say something about Krishnamurti in the present book. What we have learned makes it abundantly clear that his views are fundamentally the same as those we have been putting forward in the present volume, although they are presented in a somewhat different form and possibly from a somewhat different angle. We introduced this student of Krishnamurti to Dr. Nicoll's *Commentaries,* and he was the first to admit that they were aiming at precisely the same as Krishnamurti. As we have no wish to be accused of misinterpreting Krishnamurti in any way, we have prevailed upon our friend, a constant disciple of Krishnamurti for well over thirty years, to set down the main points of Krishnamurti's talks and writings. We shall now give these in his own words, and then invite the reader to see to what extent they agree with the Gurdjieff system.

"I am giving you what I consider are the basic points of K.'s communications (not teachings). Teachings imply something to be remembered, something to be done, something to be believed in, something to accept or reject, something for the 'formulative' mind to hang on to. Communications can induce *real* listening, induce the ability to see new significances, see new implications, receive new intimations . . . from a level *beyond* the formulative mind, beyond and outside the FIELD of thought. Let us agree to say that K. *communicates* with us, and according to our ability to listen and experience as we listen, we find our centre of consciousness functioning—i.e., either within the field of thought (memory) or beyond this field where understanding takes the place of mental pictures or suppositions.

"Now for the salient points contained in his communications. Here are some :

I. "Individuals, the world over, singly and collectively, are faced with problems which have no solution of a permanent nature. Each one is in conflict.

II. "There is no realization on the part of those who are seeking a solution that the 'I', 'Ego' or 'me' in each case is *that* responsible for the problem, in part or wholly.

III. "The failure on part of the enquirer or seeker to discover this, confines him to the limits of his own field of thought (memory) for any remedy or solution. This can only lead to some modification of conditioning for the individual or for the mass. Here, K. declares, that until the mind is free from all conditioning, there *must* BE PROBLEMS. So, to find out for oneself that which is true in any situation or circumstance, to find out what is Real, what is God, the mind must be free from *all* conditioning.

IV. "K. points out most emphatically that until the mind is aware of its own process, until it sees itself functioning in a particular pattern and is able to be free from that conditioning, obviously all search is vain. Hence it is of the greatest importance to begin with ourselves. K. repeats that it is only the mind that is capable of observing patiently its own conditioning, and, being free from its conditioning, is able to start a revaluation or radical transformation and discover that which is infinitely *beyond* the mind—beyond desire—beyond vanity and pursuits.

V. "This pin-points the absolute necessity for self-knowledge. K. declares that without self-knowledge, without knowing oneself as one is and not as one would like to be, without knowing the ways of inner thinking, all one's motives, one's thoughts, one's innumerable responses, *it is not possible* to understand and go beyond this whole process of thinking.

VI. "To quote K. from a recent talk: 'And so it is important to understand oneself, is it not? Self-knowledge is the beginning of wisdom. Self-knowledge is not according to some psychologist's book or philosopher, but to know oneself as one is from moment to moment. To know oneself is to observe what one thinks, how one feels, not just superficially, but to be deeply aware of what *is,* without condemnation, without judgment, without evaluation or comparison. Unless this takes place, not only at the superficial level, but right through the whole content of consciousness, there can be no delving into the profundity of the mind. *Please* if you are really here to understand what is being said it *is THIS* that we are concerned with and NOTHING ELSE. The mind is conditioned right through, there is no part of the mind which is not conditioned and our problem is, can such a mind free itself?' (End of quote).

VII. "The quest of self-knowledge can only take place in the field of relationship with things, people and ideas in the spheres of sex, work and society. Each moment of time we are being constantly challenged, stimulated or depressed by some impact from the environment. It is in the reaction to the impact that we have the opportunity to reveal ourselves to ourselves, to see ourselves as we are and not as we would like to be.

VIII. "The first three realizations we may experience may well be:

(a) "That we *never* think—we only recall some part of memory to deal with the challenge striking our senses from the environment.

(b) "That we never make any conscious decision regarding action. Again, some part of memory decides *for us* what we do.

(c) "That therefore we are incapable of making conscious action since some fragment of memory decides *for us* just what or what not to do. That the thinker and his thoughts are *one*. This means that we are all automatic, mechanical, repetitive, or in a state of self-hypnosis—constantly obliged to meet the present with the past, and never able to see a fact of relationship as a fact. K.'s communication to the world is that this state can be brought to an end by the individual who will give the time, interest and energy to the search. By his (K.'s) living presence he has shown that a new state of consciousness is possible, that a mind liberated from conditioning can be experienced; that all pain, sorrow and disease are the results of our intentions in relationship; and above all, that we alone can save ourselves.

"Throughout his communications K. has spoken of self-awareness leading to self-knowledge, and self-knowledge as necessary to right-thinking. Note that K. defines right-thinking as '*passive awareness of what is*', and has nothing to do with our so-called thinking, which is but recollecting some fragment of that contained within memory, when challenged by our environment. For this passive awareness to function, a state of 'unforced stillness' must be present in the mind—i.e., the mind must of its own volition be completely *un*-occupied. It seems that nothing but the realization that the mind is *completely inadequate* in dealing with any problem or search for Truth in any angle of relationship, will be sufficient for the attention to leave the field of thought (memory) and watch for significances and implications contained within the experience. K. points out that we do not have to act upon Truth, but rather Truth will act upon us.

"So throughout K.'s communications you cannot find methods, techniques, lessons, precepts, do's or don't's, because all these are appertaining to that factor in consciousness which must cease to function, if Truth, God, Love, or Reality is to come into being. It is pointed out that self-knowledge leads to practical wisdom, which means the capacity to see Truth and the ability to carry it into action, free from the compulsion of memory.

"The purpose of existence is seen to be the finding out for oneself—independent of all authorities, how the mind thinks, functions and operates; and then, go beyond it. It seems that Truth can only be found in the full cycle of challenge and response only known in relationship, from moment to moment. K. once said : 'When the mind is choicelessly aware that it *is* conditioned in this awareness, there comes a state which is not conditioned.'

"Now how do we, the 'average person', measure up against this NEW state which K. describes as 'creative'?

I. "We appear to be sound asleep, mechanical, and automatic in our responses and reactions.

II. "We appear to act under the compulsion of our memory, the end results of which are entirely unpredictable.

III. "We cannot see Truth anyhow, anywhere, or at any time. We can only *re*act mentally or emotionally according to our own conditioned memory or background.

IV. "We can find no permanent solution of our problems, individually or collectively.

V. "We cannot find uninterrupted happiness. We only experience joy and sorrow alternating.

VI. "We live and have our being within the world of opposites, from which we are obliged to choose with no Truth to guide us.

VII. "We are in conflict individually and collectively, and eventually set in motion all wars that take place. We are our own executioners.

"Although there are no precepts, techniques or methods contained in K.'s communications, there are innumerable significances and implications contained in his concepts which can be seen when the mind is still. If the seeing leads to experimental living and a revolution or radical transformation in the way of life, then K. has been responsible for leading yet another to that first and last freedom : the freedom from the conditioned mind."

The foregoing quotations can be regarded as a general analysis of Krishnamurti's teachings (or "communications"), and the reader will see many points whereon K. and the system we have presented in the present book have very much in common. They aim at the same objective albeit perhaps in somewhat different terms, and possibly from a somewhat different basis. But the basic similarity is too strong to be overlooked. The one big difference between the approach of K. and that of the Gurdjieff system is that Krishnamurti concentrates exclusively on the individual man or woman without any reference to that individual's place in the Cosmic Scheme of Things, whereas the Gurdjieff system avers that man is an essential part of the Universe and cannot be understood apart from that relationship. Therefore Cosmology plays a very important part in the system, showing how man is linked to the Cosmos, and pointing out his position in the general scheme of things.

In the book, *In Search of the Miraculous,* there are some very important diagrams dealing with this side of the subject; and in Dr. Nicoll's *Commentaries,* too. We ourselves feel that the universal aspect ought not to be neglected in man's search for self-knowledge, because the more man finds out about himself the more does he realise how closely he is linked with the Cosmos, within which "he lives and moves and has his being"; and, conversely, the more man discovers about the Universe outside himself, the more does this help him to find out about what is inside him. Because the one is the reverse of the other, man being the "microcosm" and the Universe the "macrocosm", the two being really the two sides of the same penny, as it were.

Krishnamurti no doubt has his own very good reasons for ignoring the Cosmos and concentrating exclusively upon man, and he keeps on reiterating that we have all knowledge and truth inside us. It only requires our concentration upon ourselves in the manner he depicts (and as indicated in the letter we quote) for this knowledge and truth to be made increasingly aware to us. But we ourselves still think that this lack of reference to the Cosmos is a defect in Krishnamurti's presentations, although we are fully aware that in saying this we may likely bring down the wrath of his many disciples upon our luckless head !

We also think it is important to point out here that because Krishnamurti says that we must get beyond the mind to understand reality, and that the mind is "the slayer of the real" and the great stumbling-block to real wisdom, etc., many Krishnamurti students seem to take this to mean that we must always distrust the mind and never seek to use it properly. This, of course, is the greatest of mistakes. Our minds are given us to use, and they have a very important part to play in our lives, as indicated in the chapter on "The Limitations of Logical Thinking". It is one thing to be aware of the mind's limitations, and to know of the pitfalls associated with too much concentration on the mind for inner guidance and understanding, etc.; and quite another thing to seek to disregard the mind entirely and feel that it has always to be mistrusted—because it is always likely to lead us astray. It is quite possible to appreciate fully the limitations of mind and yet make the fullest possible use of it in the spheres wherein it can be of the greatest value to man; and we feel that many Krishnamurti students do not seem to appreciate this fact. Much to their own retardation of inner development, we are afraid.

Finally, we feel we ought to say something about "teachers" in the present chapter, too. Krishnamurti is always warning his followers about "teachers" and always avers that he himself is not a "teacher", which has caused many of his followers to have something of a "bee in their bonnets" about the word. It is quite true that, as Krishnamurti says, the only real teacher is ourselves, and that we have to look within for guidance; yet, at the same time, there are people who can help us in this quest. If we tend to regard such guides as "teachers" it surely does no harm, so long as we realize that it is only we ourselves who can do the actual work of seeking our own salvation through self-knowledge, and cannot expect such "teachers" to do it for us.

It is in this light that the writer regards Gurdjieff, Ouspensky and Nicoll; they can point the way which we have to travel in our search for self-knowledge, and can give us many useful hints which can help us on in our quest. Therefore, to refuse to take such assistance from them, merely because they can be regarded as "teachers" in this special context seems to us to be rather like throwing away the baby with the bath-water! Why not gladly take advantage of the priceless assistance they have to offer, knowing that ultimately they can only point the way and that it is we ourselves who have to do the real work? Surely such an attitude is by far the most sensible one? Why not take gladly from all who can give us help in our search for self-knowledge, and be duly grateful?

It is not our purpose to say anything more about Krishnamurti, as the book is not about him, primarily; but we do think it is important to point out that Krishnamurti himself is a living embodiment of many of the ideas put forward in the present volume. He is someone who has very largely cast off the personality and lives more closely to REAL "I" than the vast majority of people.*

* Krishnamurti speaks and communicates from that dimension *beyond the mind* where the (HIS) consciousness is *established*, hence his ability to describe all and everything which lies in the Rational objective mind below it. He *is* "reflectivity" in person. (This statement is appended at the suggestion of the writer responsible for the main material of the present chapter.)

CHAPTER XXI

Is It Worth It?

WE have now come to the concluding chapter of this book, which has been an attempt to acquaint the reader with the basic ideas of the Gurdjieff system of esoteric development. We have also made some references to the communications of Krishnamurti, because we feel their aim is identical with those of the system, although using a somewhat different approach. Having given the reader a brief, though, perhaps, somewhat complicated insight into a way of thinking and living which may be diametrically opposed to what he or she has hitherto thought to be the aims and objectives of existence, the question it is now relevant to ask is : IS IT WORTH IT? Does the reader feel that what is required of him or her in the task of recreating their lives anew, is really worth while?

Naturally, everyone must answer this vital question for themselves. Presumably, the reader would not have read so far if not seeking something more deep and purposeful than the ideas about life to be found in current thought generally. It is only those dissatisfied with what life has had to offer them hitherto, or with the ideas and generalisations about the meaning and purpose of existence that reading and thinking have brought to them, who would have been at all keen to read a book such as the present one. Therefore, we feel that such people are essentially the right type of material for the task of esoteric (or inner) development. Being dissatisfied both with themselves and what they have made of life to date, they can see now—as a result of reading the present book—how they have gone astray in their understanding of the problem in hand. They have never realized before that the key to the whole situation is to *know themselves,* that self-knowledge is the basis for all real inner development and the achievement of real wisdom.

It is so easy to remain as one is and just add this or that new idea or thought to one's stock of previously garnered ideas and views. It is so fatally easy to lose oneself in this or that "ism" or cult, and think that one is "making progress". But nothing really worth-while can ever be achieved unless we realize that *we have got to change ourselves;* that we have got to become *different people from those we now are.* For this most radical of changes to be effected, it is vitally essential that we should begin forthwith on the task of understanding what we really are, what it is that "makes us tick". We have got to know ourselves, in all our stark reality, with all our faults and failings, our love of self (i.e., a self which is not our real self but prevents us from knowing the reality within us). All this we have got to discover. The more light we can throw upon ourselves and our real motives, attitudes, emotions, etc., the more surely will we begin to gradually come awake, out of the sleep of the personality in which we have been encased all our lives. We have got to wake up and live, and that means getting away from the hypnotism of the self we thought we were, but which is only an illusion which prevents us from knowing what we really are. We think we are what we are not, and until we know this, we can never begin to become what we really are (and were intended to be).

In this task of real creation, i.e., the re-creation of ourselves, only real esoteric knowledge can help us; and the system indicated in this book can give us the greatest possible assistance in achieving our objective. If the reader is vitally interested, he or she should read Ouspensky's *In Search of the Miraculous,* for a fuller understanding of the system; and they should also study Dr. Maurice Nicoll's five volumes of *Psychological Commentaries on the teachings of Gurdjieff and Ouspensky.* These offer endless opportunity for work on oneself in the light they throw on the basic teachings of THE WORK.

But one does not work on oneself merely for personal reasons. In the first place, it is not ourself that gains by our efforts—at least not the self we have been used to. That is the victim of The Work efforts we have to make in order to allow REAL "I" to come into existence in our lives and transfigure and transform them. But, further than this, we have to work with others likewise interested in working on themselves, so that our joint efforts can help all concerned. In the system we have discussed, work is usually done in groups. There are groups working in this way scattered about the world, so we not only work on ourselves, but we work with others in The Work, in groups, so that all may benefit jointly.

There is yet a further reason for carrying out the teachings of The Work, and that is to further The Work itself. If we strive to obey this threefold idea of work on ourselves, work with others, and work for the sake of The Work, then our efforts are thrice-blessed. This threefold basis of working prevents us from concentrating too much on ourselves and our own "advancement". Concentrating on ourselves can so easily tend to fortify and strengthen that self-love which is the chief antagonist we have; so that, instead of working for its overthrow, as we thought, we find that we have merely added to its power over us. This underlines the need for assistance in trying to carry out The Work teachings, and the desirability of working with a group and under the direction of someone skilled in the application of the system.

Naturally, it takes years of work on oneself to get to know anything real about ourselves; we may think we are finding out a great deal, through self-observation and by applying the other teachings and techniques of The Work, briefly referred to in the present volume. What we think we have discovered about ourselves is very superficial at first, so that real self-knowledge only comes after years of patient effort. But such effort is immensely worth while in every particular, because it not only transforms us, it transforms our whole life for us; because as our level of being changes, so does our life change, too. We become different people *inside,* and this is reflected by the way life treats us *outside.*

That is an esoteric law briefly referred to in previous pages, and explains why it is only ourselves who can make anything really worthwhile of our lives. It is no good looking to external factors or agencies to do this for us. Such things cannot change our level of being, and so life remains just as it was before, despite whatever we may be doing or thinking. It is only when we begin to really work on ourselves, and change our habitual ways of thinking and feeling, that anything real or permanent can happen to us. For self-change is the basic pre-requisite for external change. And self-change can only come about as a result of self-knowledge and work on oneself.

Let us conclude this book with a personal note. The writer has been deeply interested in what is known as "deeper thought" for the whole of his adult life. In his early twenties he was an avid student of philosophy, psychology, literature, economics, etc., at Toynbee Hall, in the East End of London, under the auspices of the Workers Educational Association, and for some years had the late C. E. M. Joad as his tutor. He became an ardent socialist and "reformer" as a result of all that he read and heard and pondered over. At about this time fate brought him into touch with Theosophy (which is the Western name for the Ancient Wisdom of the East). Under this influence he began to realize that most of what Western people thought about "reform" and "progress" were really only superficial things after all. They sought to change people from outside, i.e., by altering conditions and affording them better opportunities for self-expression, etc. The writer came to realize—as a result of his study of Theosophy—that real change can only come from within oneself; and unless there was this inner change it did not matter how much was done by others to change the conditions and amenities of outer existence for us. That did not solve one's problems in living. It might change their form and content, but the basic problems still remained, and defied solution, simply because they were not being faced in the right way. So that "isms", such as Socialism or Communism, really did not get down to basic realities.

The writer had concluded many years previously that orthodox religions had no answer to the basic problems of life; and he also had come to realize that science and materialism had no answer, either. In Theosophy he found at last what he had been seeking for, in the way of an understanding of the meaning and purpose of life. But after many years as a theosophist he felt he still had not found the final key, and although he had made great changes in his mode of thinking as a result of his theosophical knowledge, there was something which still eluded him. It was only when he came in touch with the *Commentaries* of Dr. Nicoll that he discovered the missing key. That key was self-knowledge.

It is true that in theosophical literature this teaching is to be found; but the writer feels that it is not presented in a way in which many can understand it. It is couched in terms and covered in phrases which tend to throw one off the scent, unless one is fortunate enough to have someone as teacher who can direct one's footsteps aright. The writer will forever feel grateful to that *Karma* which put the *Commentaries* in his way. In a sense he feels that in some small measure he is repaying that debt by writing the present book. If it succeeds in bringing only a few into The Work, he feels the effort entailed in writing it will have been fully justified. He has not abandoned his Theosophy. The Work teachings only serve to deepen and widen his understanding of the basic theosophical concepts, and *vice versa*.

Also, he thinks it only fair to comment here that in his view the Cosmology which Theosophy puts before one is wider and deeper, in many respects, than that put forward in the Gurdjieff system. Be that as it may, as a result of what Theosophy and The Work have brought him, the writer feels that the complete solution to the problem of existence has been vouchsafed him. And who, indeed, could expect or hope for more? The only thing that remains is to apply that knowledge and understanding in one's life, so that as each year passes one comes ever-closer to the heart of things; for, as self-knowledge increases through work on oneself, so does one's understanding of life in general expand, taking more and more of the Cosmos in its embrace. One knows more about oneself; about what one really is; and, as a direct corollary, one knows more about the world outside oneself, too. The one type of knowledge is the obverse of the other.

Thus, as self-knowledge increases and deepens, so one's wisdom and understanding about life in general increases and deepens. One feels, therefore, that having been given so much, it is only right to try to share one's riches with others, and that is why people who are in The Work try to tell others about it. But only those who are really ready will respond. Others will listen, perhaps, and may even be interested superficially; but *really* they are not. They fall back into their old sloth and indifference, or chase after this or that new cult or "ism" in the belief that here, at last, is what they have been seeking all this time. Only to be disillusioned once again, of course, in due time. But those with Magnetic Centre (briefly referred to in this book), and who are ready for what The Work has to offer will be immediately attracted to it when once it has been brought to their attention. In this context the writer sincerely hopes this book will play some part in stirring up interest in the subject. Surely nothing could be of greater importance to the real seeker than to be given the chance to contact The Work? And it is with the thought that in writing this book he may have done something really concrete to help on this objective that the writer now ends his self-appointed task. The rest is up to the reader!